Clueless in the Garden

Clueless in the Garden

A Guide for the Horticulturally Helpless

Yvonne Cunnington

KEY PORTER BOOKS

Copyright © 2003 by Yvonne Cunnington

National Library of Canada Cataloguing in Publication

Cunnington, Yvonne
Clueless in the garden: a guide for the horticulturally helpless / Yvonne Cunnington

(The Clueless series)
Includes index.
ISBN 1-55263-409-4

1. Gardening. I. Title. II. Series: Clueless series.

SB450.97.C87 2002   635   C2002-905366-8

The publisher gratefully acknowledges the support of the Canada Council for the Arts and the Ontario Arts Council for its publishing program.

We acknowledge the financial support of the Government of Canada through the Book Publishing Industry Development Program (BPIDP) for our publishing activities.

Key Porter Books Limited
70 The Esplanade
Toronto, Ontario
Canada M5E 1R2

www.keyporter.com

Text design: Jack Steiner
Cover and text illustrations: Peter Cook
Electronic formatting: Jean Lightfoot Peters

Printed and bound in Canada

03 04 05 06 07 08 6 5 4 3 2 1

To my mother, who ensured that I would never be entirely clueless in the garden.

Contents

Acknowledgments

Thank you to Marjorie Harris, who put me up to this, and to the editors at *Chatelaine* and *Gardening Life*, who commissioned articles that became the nuclei for several chapters. For expert horticultural guidance, I'm grateful to my friends Sandy Perry at Michigan State University, whose cheerful emails and helpful comments sustained me through writing, and Anne Marie Van Nest of the Niagara Parks Commission School of Horticulture, who kindly reviewed the manuscript. Heartfelt thanks go to my sister, Barbara Bout, who after reading the manuscript is no longer clueless in the garden, and to my husband, John, whose energy and support makes everything possible.

ICONS

You'll find these symbols scattered throughout the book. Here's what they mean:

Best Bets

Helpful Hint

How To...

Earth-Friendly Tip

Time-Saver

Money-Saver

Chapter 1

Rolling Up Your Sleeves: How to Get Started

You look out the window and there it is: Your bare, neglected, over-grown (circle the one that applies) yard yawns before you. Visions of perennial borders, sun-ripened tomatoes, and fragrant flowering shrubs tempt you, but you know that anything you plant is doomed—you weren't around the day they passed out the green thumbs.

Even if you knew what to plant—and that's a big enough hurdle—you wouldn't know where, how, or when. And as for that weedy, compacted, tree-root-infested, muddy—or dusty—dirt you've got, won't any plant just turn up its toes anyway? Besides, isn't it *a lot of work*?

Well, yes, work is a four-letter word—but you can have a garden and a life too, and no, it's not too late to grow a green thumb. Actually, as one of my favorite garden wits, the acerbic Henry Mitchell, once put it, "There are no green thumbs or black thumbs. There are only gardeners and non-gardeners. Gardeners are the ones who ruin after ruin get on with the high defiance of nature herself, creating, in the very face of her chaos and tornado, the bower of roses and the pride of irises."

So relax, take a deep breath; help has arrived. No, I'm not coming over to help you dig your flower beds—I've got my own garden, thank you very much—but this book is the next best thing. Stay with it to find out what you need to know. But don't get too hung up on to-do lists. The main reason starter gardeners fail has less to do with being clueless than with the fact that they don't pay enough attention to their gardens. Yes, you need to know the how, why, and when stuff—but even more important, you need to get outside. That way, you're more likely to notice if the seedlings are getting parched or something's been chewing your favorite shrub or that Vigorous New Perennial is overtaking everything in sight. Noticing these things while there's still time to do something about them is one of the keys to success. And the more time you spend in the garden, the sooner you'll figure out what works for you and what doesn't.

No, this doesn't mean moving into the garden shed during the growing season. Just pay your garden a visit several times a week and really look at what's going on—what's growing well, what needs a nip

---

The Ho-Mi (or EZ) digger

I discovered this handy tool after a bout of bad wrist strain from gardening and working on a computer keyboard, and it's so much easier to use that I don't bother with trowels anymore.

One type looks like a ploughshare on the end of a short wooden handle, or you can get one with a long, hoe-like handle—I use both. The hand-sized variety does everything a trowel can do, but a whole lot better. Using a trowel, you have to twist your wrist. After planting a couple of flats of impatiens, you notice the strain. With the Ho-Mi digger, you simply make a couple of up and down motions while pulling it toward you and you've got your planting hole. It's a lot quicker too. I use the longer-handled model like a plough to make rows when I'm planting seeds or setting out onion or garlic bulbs.

If your garden center doesn't carry this tool, many mail order seed catalogues sell it.

and a tuck, and, oh, better pull out that weed right now before it goes to seed.

As for the work part, I call it "playing in the garden." Self-deception? I don't think so. Gardening should be fun—it's really creative play. There's enormous pleasure to be had growing things and putting good-looking plants together—gardening is a bit like matchmaking, you know. And what's wrong with losing a few pounds digging? I'd rather burn calories while getting a chance to smell the flowers and watch robins splash in the bird bath than on a dreary treadmill at the gym.

So you want to turn your boring yard into a garden? Great, let's get started.

First you're going to need some tools.

Tools of the Trade

A lot of the stuff that promises to make gardening easier just ends up cluttering the garden shed. There are plenty of garden gizmos that you're safe to ignore. Here's a hint: If a tool is too pretty to get dirty, you don't need it. Half a dozen basic tools should cover most jobs— and if that's all you need, you can afford to buy quality, right?

Good tools make the difference between frustration and enjoyment, or at least the satisfaction of getting the work (oops, I mean the play) done. If you're cursing because the pruner won't cut, the spade's handle has broken off, and your new hose leaks already, gardening *does* seem like a lot of trouble.

Buying quality versions of the following essential person-powered implements shouldn't break the bank.

For cutting and pruning

- You'll need **hand-held pruning shears** for light shrub and rose pruning and cutting back perennials. Look for a bypass model (which has a curved blade that passes by a fixed base) for clean cuts that don't pinch stems. Also look for forged steel blades, a strong spring, and comfortable handles.
- **Lopping pruners** have longer handles and bigger blades for cutting more substantial branches. Like hand pruners, a bypass cutting head is best.

This happens to me all the time: I'm in the garden and I put down the tool I'm using, then I see something else that needs attention—then I can't find my tool. A friend of mine, a professional landscaper, had the perfect solution: He spray-painted the wooden handles of all his shovels, rakes, and hand tools bright yellow so no matter where he puts them down, they stand out. Now, there's an idea worth copying.

For digging, turning, and moving soil

- A good **spade** and **shovel** make digging almost a pleasure. Look for forged metal heads and handles that fit securely into the shaft. Hardwood handles should have a varnished finish, fit comfortably in your hands, and feel like the right weight for you (they shouldn't feel overly heavy). A spade has a narrow, long blade that is ideal for working in flower beds, but it's also worth buying a rounded shovel for making larger planting holes for trees and shrubs.
- Once you've effectively broken the ground, a **digging fork** is good for breaking up soil clods, but it's really an option.
- A **hand trowel** is useful for digging small holes for planting annuals and vegetable plants—or try the tool I use instead, the **Ho-Mi digger**, sometimes called **EZ digger**. (See box on page 14.)

For raking

You'll need a **stiff-tined rake** for leveling soil and removing small stones, plus a **fan-style rake** to clean up fall leaves.

For watering

- Buy a **garden hose** that has brass fittings and is at least three to four ply in thickness. When not in use, keep your hose coiled and hung up and remove kinks promptly.
- A **watering wand** is the perfect tool for watering seedlings, new plantings, and container gardens—it has a handle that's long enough for watering hanging baskets and the nozzle has many tiny holes that deliver water in a soft shower rather than a strong pressurized stream. Look for one with a brass rather than plastic shutoff valve.
- You need a good **sprinkler** for the lawn, and consider **soaker hoses** for your garden beds. (Read more about these in Chapter 4.)

For weeding

- A standard **hoe** is useful when weeds are very small. A **hand-held circle hoe** is a neat gizmo with a short wooden handle and a sharp

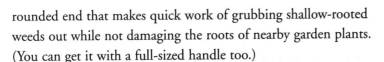

rounded end that makes quick work of grubbing shallow-rooted weeds out while not damaging the roots of nearby garden plants. (You can get it with a full-sized handle too.)

- Slip a **weeding knife** close to the stem of dandelions and other weeds, then move it toward the plant, and loosen the soil around the roots so you can flip or pull the weed out, roots and all, in a couple of deft moves. You'll have to experiment to find what works best for you. I used to use a retired kitchen knife, which did double duty as a perennial divider until its blade broke, but now I swear by my Japanese farmer's knife (which has a wide blade about 7" [18 cm] long) from Lee Valley Tools.

Nice to have too

Wheelbarrow or garden cart, 100' (30 m) tape measure, shears for trimming hedges or clipping grass, a pruning saw for larger branches, a decent pair of scissors relegated to garden use, and a Swiss army knife.

For the power tool brigade

The larger your place, the more tempting the following tools—at least until you get a peek at the price tag, because here's where things get seriously expensive. Fortunately most small plots are easy to tend without them, or you can consider renting when necessary.

- **Power mower:** Most everybody has one, but if you hate the noise they make, the new improved reel mowers are popular with people who have very small lawns.
- **String trimmer:** When you get tired of edging beds by hand.
- **Leaf blower:** Takes the fun out of raking leaves, doesn't it?
- **Leaf shredder:** I wouldn't mind one of these.
- **Rototiller:** Handy only if you have a very large garden.

Make Yourself Comfortable

Other can't-live-without items include a gardener's kneeling pad. It's more comfortable than strap-on kneepads, which bite into the back of your legs (and look dorky as well).

Good gloves are also essential—and thank goodness glove manufacturers have finally figured out that women need decent work gloves too! I can't stand the thin cotton types with little plastic dots all over the fingers and palms; instead, I get light, good-quality leather gloves at a place that sells work clothes. These may be a bit more expensive, but, hey, I'm worth it.

I recently discovered a gardener's tool belt with loops for pruners, the weeding knife, and the Ho-Mi digger, and large pockets that will hold all the odds and sods that you're constantly running around looking for: string, plant tags, marker pen, seed packets, you name it. Great invention—haven't carpenters had their own version for eons? A variation on the theme is a similar apron-style gizmo that you slip over a metal bucket and take around the garden with you.

Finally, always use sunscreen and slip on a hat. A good straw hat will at least help you look the part, even though you may not quite feel like a gardener yet. Don't worry—stick with it and you will!

Chapter 2

Climate Control: Gardening Where You Live

Gardeners can be forgiven for being obsessed with the weather—it comes with the territory. But we can be real party-poopers: While the unenlightened enjoy endless sunshine, gardeners are fretting that it hasn't rained in more than a month. Just ignore us as we tend to the watering—better still, offer us a stiff drink and condolences.

On the love/hate relationship gardeners have with the weather, the late Henry Mitchell, author of *The Essential Earthman,* wasn't one to mince words: "It is not nice to garden anywhere," he wrote. "Everywhere there are violent winds, startling once-per-five-centuries floods, unprecedented droughts, record-setting freezes, abusive and blasting heats never known before. There is no place, no garden, where these terrible things do not drive gardeners mad."

As Mitchell well knew, climate is the wild card affecting our gardens. Long-term temperature and precipitation patterns, how far north you are, the direction of prevailing winds, distance from major bodies of water, and local topography all influence what will grow well for you and what isn't worth trying.

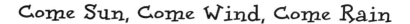

Come Sun, Come Wind, Come Rain

When you start to take more than a passing interest in the vital stats of your climate, you're on your way to becoming a gardener. If you measure how much rain falls, you won't get taken in if there isn't enough to get a duck wet. For plants, that kind of rain amounts to a dust settler that doesn't get moisture to the roots where it's needed.

If you live in a region where temperatures go below freezing, you'll need to know the average last frost date in spring—the date it's normally safe to plant frost-tender annuals and tomatoes—and also the first frost in the fall, when those same tender plants turn to mush. The period in between—the growing season—is what plants (and many people) need to strut their stuff.

And if you're keen to grow veggies, the number of frost-free days your region gets will determine what plants you can grow. Tomatoes, for example, need a long season, while other crops, such as peas, mature much more quickly. Plant breeders have helped short-season gardeners out by coming up with strains of tomatoes such as "Early Girl" that ripen more quickly.

Keeping tabs on the weather

Recording rainfall and noting first and last frosts is a great habit to get into so you'll know when to do extra watering or run out to cover the annuals. I record this information on the kitchen calendar. To help you figure out what's really going on, you need:

- **An outdoor thermometer:** Place it out of direct sun to get accurate readings. The new wireless thermometers let you put the sensor outdoors but read temperatures in the comfort of your kitchen.
- **A rain gauge:** If you record the amount of rainfall, you'll always know when to get out the sprinkler and when to sit back and relax. Most plants are happiest with 1" (25 mm) of rain a week.

A Hardy Plant is Good to Find

How do you know which plants will "winter over" in your garden? This is where the horticultural ("hort" to its friends) term "hardiness zone" comes in. Plants that are *hardy* to your region are those that routinely survive the lowest temperatures and whatever else winter throws at them. What's more, they do this *without artificial protection.*

I know someone who grows a fig tree in Toronto, but he accomplishes this by protecting the tree with an elaborate plywood shelter that he fills with leaves for insulation. He erects his fig house every fall and takes it down in the spring. Most of us aren't going to go to that kind of trouble—nor do we need to. There are plenty of plants that will survive winter on their own.

A hardiness zone describes an area with a similar number of frost-free days and average low temperatures. But it isn't just how frigid the winter gets that affects what plants will thrive for you, it's the sum total of regional weather patterns—rain, wind, sun, summer heat and humidity, and winter snow cover—as well as how weather interacts with your topography. Nearby big bodies of water, for example, help to moderate temperatures.

Zoning in on plant hardiness

There are several maps showing hardiness zones, but most gardeners in North America rely on the U.S. Department of Agriculture's plant hardiness zone map, used by most American gardening sources, or the Agriculture Canada zone map. The USDA zone map includes Canada and bases its zones on minimum winter temperatures. The Canadian map is based on a wider array of meteorological and horticultural information, especially observations of what plants grow where, but doesn't include the U.S. Some Canadian books employ the homegrown map, while others use USDA data or include both. When you're looking at a gardening book, it will usually tell you which system the author uses (this book uses USDA zones).

For both zone maps, here's the bottom line:

- Just like a thermometer, the higher the number, the warmer the region. For example, a plant rated as hardy to zone 5 is not recommended for the colder zones 4 to 1.
- If you're Canadian, it helps to know both the Canadian and USDA zone you live in because many plants imported from the U.S. have tags listing the USDA hardiness zone and these zone numbers are usually one lower. For example, if you garden in Canadian zone 6, as I do, your USDA hardiness is zone 5.

DID YOU KNOW?

- Hardiness is genetic. Some plants are naturally more tolerant of cold temperatures than others, and some cultivars of the same plant may be hardier because they were bred or selected from plants found to be tougher than their cousins.
- The hardiness zone number will help you decide which woody plants will grow in your climate. When it comes to perennials, however, many experienced gardeners find they can grow plants that books say aren't hardy in their region. For example, winter rain, ice, and freeze-thaw patterns can often kill plants in milder regions that do fine in northerly regions, where plants are insulated by a thick blanket of snow all winter long.
- Gardeners in the colder regions are often green with envy because their southern counterparts can grow plants like camellias outdoors. But there is some consolation: Many plants—and people too—sulk in extreme heat and humidity, and other plants, such as peonies and daffodils, need a period of cold weather or they won't bloom. This limits what gardeners can plant in the hot and humid American south. The American Horticultural Society has come to the rescue and developed a heat zone map to help southern gardeners determine what plants they can grow. (On the Internet, see **www.ahs.org/garden/gdnheatmap.htm** for details.)

Bringing the big picture down to your garden

Hardiness zone ratings are intended only as a guide. Some people get "zoneitis"—being afraid to try plants that might be a bit iffy—while others, like the fig grower in Toronto, live in zone denial.

Generally, if you have sheltered areas in the garden or if you provide winter protection, you can extend the range of some plants by one zone. Plants near the house may be in a warmer zone because heat is escaping from or absorbed by the building. A south-facing slope will be warmer than nearby level areas. If hedges protect your garden, you may be successful with plants that a neighbor on a windswept hill can't grow.

Remember, plants don't read books. Many gardeners discover they can grow species that books say won't work for them, so take zone ratings with a grain of salt. And of course a plant might fail for other reasons as well: It might not like the texture or chemistry of your soil (see page 25), the light, or the moisture levels in your garden. All gardeners kill some plants some of the time. You will too, and you'll get over it. (There's no better excuse to try a new plant.)

Shade in midsummer

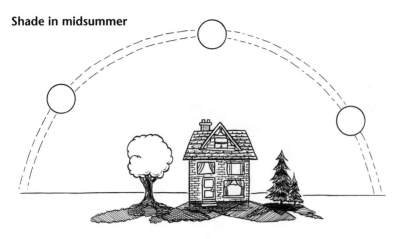

Shade in winter

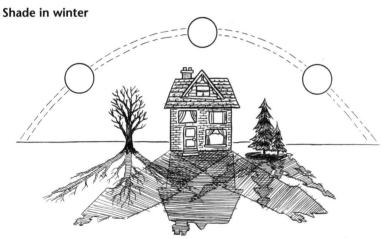

Your garden gets more shade in winter, spring, and fall, when the sun is lower in the sky.

Which Way Does the Sun Shine?

The exposure of your garden—where north, south, east, and west are situated—has a lot to do with the light levels your plants will be getting. Watch where the sun rises and sets. Keep in mind:

• The position of the sun changes depending on the time of year, so a shady corner in winter may be sunny in summer or vice versa. I once planted shade-loving hostas in a spot that was shady—at least in the spring. By midsummer, it got such intense sun at mid-day that the leaves were sunburned. The moral? Find out where and

when the sun shines on your property before making planting decisions.

- Whether your garden is shaded and the kind of shade you get will also play a role in your plant choices. But this isn't carved in stone either. You can change light patterns by cutting a tree down or at least thinning out branches, and you can plant trees or build a structure to provide shade. (For more on shade gardening, see Chapter 9.)

Chapter 3

Breaking Ground: Soil 101

When you moved into your house, the dirt in your yard came with it. But now that you're gardening, let's use a more dignified four-letter word. Soil. You'll get *dirt* under your nails, but *soil* is the phenomenal substance at the foundation of your garden.

So what is soil really? It's actually a lot of stuff working together. The combination of everything listed below is what makes soil *alive*.

- **Rock particles:** Over millions of years, rocks get broken down into finer and finer mineral particles, and these particles largely determine the texture of your soil. The largest particles give you sandy soil, medium-sized particles give you silty soil, and very small particles give you clay.

- **Organic matter, or humus:** This is hort-speak for the end product of nature's impressive recycling scheme—decayed remains of plants, animals, and manure. Happily for us, by the time it's called "humus" (a term not to be confused with mashed chickpeas), all that rotted stuff isn't the least bit yucky. It smells earthily pleasant and resembles rich, dark soil. Humus creates a loose soil structure that holds moisture and air and drains well. Each fall, the cycle renews itself as leaves drop and vegetation dies back. In nature, this stuff doesn't get cut back and raked up; it decomposes to provide food for plants.

- **Soil critters and fungi:** No need to get squeamish here, but good soil is full of life forms—most of them microscopic—ranging from billions of bacteria and fungi to bugs, earthworms, and small burrowing mammals. These are the recyclers that convert nutrients in humus into water-soluble forms that plant roots can take up. Some fungi (called mycorrhizae) actually team up with plant roots to make nutrients available to the plants. The more life forms there are in the soil, the richer and more crumbly it is, allowing roots, air, and water to penetrate. Too much tilling and excessive dependence on pesticides and fertilizers has adverse effects on these beneficial life forms.
- **Air:** Roots don't really grow in the soil—they flourish in the air spaces among soil particles. Subterranean life forms also need to breathe so they can do their job of chomping up organic matter.
- **Water:** Water is a good thing and essential to life, but too much or too little causes problems. Water flows quickly through soil that's very sandy, making it dry out too fast, draining or leaching soil of nutrients as it percolates through. Clay soils have the opposite problem: They can easily become waterlogged as the small vital air pores fill with water, which can kill off soil organisms and destroy or injure plant roots. (Water and wetland plants are adapted to high moisture and low air content.)

Checking Out Your Soil

Take a spade and dig up a slice of soil. If you find perfect garden loam—soil that resembles crumbly chocolate cake and is easy to dig—you've won the gardener's equivalent of the lottery. Garden loam has roughly equal parts of sand, silt, and clay—the chief mineral components of soil—with about 5% organic matter, or humus, as the icing on the cake.

Your own garden soil is more likely to be sandy, silty, or clayey, but it's probably a mixture of all three with one predominating. To find

out what you've got, squeeze a handful of slightly damp soil in your fist. If it refuses to form a ball and just falls apart, chances are that you've got sandy soil. If it forms a hard, smooth ball, you're at the other end of the spectrum with clay soil. If it's in the middle, you've got loam and your luck is intact.

Take the fist test

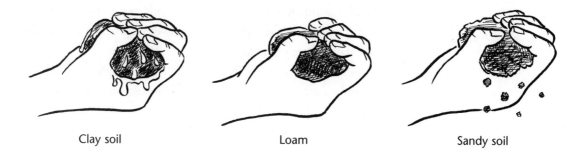

Clay soil   Loam   Sandy soil

We humans have a way of disrupting the natural cycle of decay that produces humus as we prune, mow, cut, rake, and then send the stuff off with the garbage or to the compost pile (if we've seen the light). There's no great secret to growing plants successfully: Imitate nature and regularly revitalize the soil by adding humus, and you're well on your way.

Is Your Soil on Acid? Soil pH

This sounds a bit like chemistry (well, it is, but bear with me), but soil pH is one of the factors that influences what plants you can grow well.

My philosophy is to grow plants that like my soil rather than changing its chemistry to suit the plants, and I confess that, like most gardeners, I've never tested my soil. I've been told by reliable sources that the soil pH in my region is great for growing most plants—which fortunately suits my philosophy. You may not be so lucky.

A quick overview of pH

The pH scale measures whether soil is acid or alkaline. The numbers on the scale run from 1 to 14, with neutral at pH 7. Levels below 7 are rated acidic; levels above 7 are alkaline. Most plants prefer a

slightly acidic soil pH of 6.0 to 6.5. Fortunately many soils oblige by falling within this range, but there are regions where the soil is more acid or quite alkaline, and that limits the plants that will thrive there.

Soil pH affects the nutrients available for plant growth. In some very alkaline soils (pH 8 and above), certain plants may be shut out of getting the necessary nitrogen, phosphorus, iron, and other nutrients that are dissolved in soil moisture. For example, plants like azaleas and rhododendrons need acidic soil; otherwise, they're like starving street urchins, faces pressed to the windows of the well-to-do on a feast day—so near and yet so far.

You can adjust soils to modify their pH level (though this tends to work for only a season or so). Adding lime makes acid soils more alkaline, while adding sulphur, peat, or an acidic fertilizer can help rebalance alkaline soils. To get more specific advice on what to do—and when—consult local garden experts such as Master Gardeners, county extension agents, or your garden center.

By the way, it's easier to make acidic soils more alkaline than the other way around, but it's easier still to go with the flow and grow plants naturally suited to the pH you already have.

There, now, that wasn't so bad, was it?

Before You Get Out Your Spade...

Look closely at your property and think about how you'll be using it. (See Chapter 15 for more on garden planning.) If level ground is at a premium, do you need to do some terracing and build retaining walls? If your property is rocky, will raised beds and extra soil help?

"Enough already!" you're probably thinking, "I just want a flower bed and a tomato patch, and you're talking major earthworks." The idea is not to overwhelm you, but to point out that if there's a job that involves heavy machinery, do it now or plan for it down the road. You don't really want to spend time and money undoing what you've already spent time and money doing, do you?

Making Your Bed

Doing this job right is at the heart of your garden's success. Basically it involves adding a layer of humus-rich material to the soil and digging it in. Yes, you'll work up a sweat, but besides the potential loss of a couple of pounds, there's another consolation: You have to do this only once. Really. Once the bed is in place, the only time you'll have to dig is when planting or transplanting, or if you really get into it and decide to expand.

But it is hard work. If you can't bribe a relative or friend to help, consider hiring somebody. If you're willing to wait a few months, there's even a way to prep beds that avoids the digging part altogether (see box below).

Get rid of grass and weeds

If you're planning to turn the soil in an area covered with grass or weeds, you've got to boot them both out so they won't resurface later to make gardening life miserable. First outline the area with a garden hose for curves or a string line for straight edges. View it close up and

---

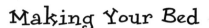

Prepping a bed that makes itself

This method takes more time because it kills the grass by smothering it over a few months, but it's a great way to avoid turning the soil and save your back too. Do this in the fall and your bed should be ready to plant by spring:

- Cut the grass at the mower's lowest setting.
- To help smother grass and weeds, spread layers of newspaper about 12 sheets thick. (They will decompose eventually.)
- Next, spread a layer of shredded leaves. (Run them over with the lawn mower or put them through a chipper-shredder before spreading. If you use them intact, they take too long to break down.) Then add about 6" (15 cm) of a mixture of topsoil and compost or manure, which you can buy at a garden center.
- Let the mound sit until spring. There's no need to turn the soil over. The soil will settle, but the bed will end up slightly raised, which is perfect for planting.

Cut squares of sod by slicing down with a flat-edged spade, then slice under the sod before lifting sod off.

from a number of angles further away (go indoors, for example, and check it out from the various rooms you look out of and whatever levels you have). Arrange and rearrange until the bed outline pleases you.

Then you can get rid of grass and perennial weeds in one of three ways: by removing them, by smothering them over several months, or by spraying a non-selective herbicide such as Roundup. By the way, "non-selective" means it kills *all* vegetation it touches, so don't spray on a windy day. To apply this type of herbicide, read and follow the label's directions. Apply just enough to wet the foliage. The grass will turn yellow within five to seven days. Despite the precautions, this is still one of the safest herbicides to use as far as the environment is concerned: There is no residual effect in the soil and you can dig and plant into the bed as soon as the grass is dead. It's safe for humans too, but make sure you follow the instructions for safe use on the label.

If you want to avoid using herbicides, follow these steps to do the job by hand:

- Mow the area on your mower's lowest setting. Then dig and slice under the sod with a flat-edged spade.
- Use the spade to cut the sod into squares, slicing down on it with the straight edge as you would when edging a bed before slicing pieces off. Slice as thin as you can—you want to leave most of top-soil.
- Dump the removed pieces of sod on the compost pile upside down so they don't start to grow there.

Never dig or till clay soil in early spring when it's wet—this will cause clay particles to press into a sticky, unworkable mass.

Enrich your soil

Most soils have been altered by human action and lack organic matter. Starter gardeners often skip the step of adding humus and then regret it after spending good money on plants that aren't happy.

Ironically, the way to improve either a heavy clay or a light sandy soil is identical—spread humus, in a layer about 2" to 3" (5 to 8 cm) thick, over the entire garden bed. In sandy soils, humus acts like a sponge to catch and hold moisture while accumulating nutrients and adding fertility. In clay soils, humus breaks up the small particles that stick together so tightly and helps create larger pore spaces that drain more easily and hold air.

What kind of humus to add? Did you ever seriously think you'd be contemplating the merits of manure? Common types found at garden centers include composted cattle or sheep manure, available bagged or in bulk. Either is good, but it should be well rotted (most manure sold at garden suppliers will be). Fresh stuff right out the barn is too strong—it can burn your plants and isn't exactly the most pleasing smell to introduce into the neighborhood.

Besides manure, ideal choices are compost (decomposed garden and kitchen waste) and leaf mold (composted leaves). You can make both in your backyard, and sometimes they are available locally if your town or city has a composting program.

What about peat moss? Peat is good for sandy soils because it too acts like a sponge. Be sure to moisten it first, though (otherwise, it can draw moisture out of the soil). And don't rely on it by itself, as it contains few nutrients and is hard to work in—add some manure or compost as well.

Dig this!

Okay, you've added a layer of humus-rich material. Here's how to work it in.

To start, dig up the soil in a line at one end of the bed, leaving a shallow trench. Take this soil to the other end of the bed in a wheelbarrow or whatever you've got that can handle it. Then turn the soil next to the trench into the trench. Do this all the way to the end: Your bed will turn out to be more level this way, and the humus you've added will be mixed in with the soil. Fill in the last trench with the soil from the first one. To avoid back strain, don't dig big clumps—aim for small slices. If you want the soil's texture to be finer, it may benefit from another turning with a garden fork to break up any large clods. If you're doing this job in the fall for spring planting, however, just leave the big clods—winter weather and frost will break them up further.

Rake the bed smooth, and call it a day.

Help!

My Garden Bed Is Huge

Rototilling is the most realistic way to work areas of more than 1,000 square feet (93 square meters). You can hire someone or rent, borrow, or buy a machine. Large, heavy tillers do the best job, effectively working at least 8" (20 cm) down. I'll do most other gardening jobs, including digging, but I always leave this chore to my husband, and he generally leaves the planting to me. Not a bad bargain, I think.

Black Magic: Making Compost for Your Garden

When I was growing up, we had a compost pile and we kids took turns taking vegetable peelings out to it. Perhaps that's why I've always thought of composting as the most natural thing in the world.

I feel guilty if I throw the smallest lemon peel into the garbage, so it surprises me that everybody with a yard doesn't compost. Remember, materials that can be composted make up 20% to 30% of household waste—that's a lot of good stuff for the garden that won't be wasted at the garbage dump.

Compost is the best treat you can give your soil. As well as enriching it and improving its texture, scientists have even discovered that compost helps protect plants from pests and diseases.

How compost happens

There are complicated recipes for making compost—enough to put anybody off getting started—but don't drive yourself crazy. Just heap stuff into a bin or onto a pile and keep it moist. The material will decompose eventually. Do make an effort to screen the operation from view: Cunningly planted evergreen shrubs will do a nice job, as will a trellis fence or a garden shed.

Composting works best when an equal balance of materials containing carbon—generally brown in color, such as autumn leaves or straw—and materials containing nitrogen—generally green, such as kitchen scraps and grass clippings—are combined. Turning the material occasionally with a pitchfork or whatever's at hand helps speed decomposition.

If you live in an urban area, it's best to use a bin. When I had a small city garden, I worked out a two-bin approach because using only one bin made it difficult to get finished compost out of the bottom while continuing to add to the top. With two bins, we could fill one over the summer and then turn that material into the second bin along with shredded leaves in the fall. Over the winter, we would refill the empty bin. By spring, the compost from the previous season was ready for the garden and we would turn the winter's material and that spring's yard waste into the empty bin, where it would "cook" through the summer and be usable by fall. This method yielded enough compost for a small garden. When we started, the soil was heavy, nasty clay, but by the time we moved, six years later, it was perfect loam.

But you can't take it with you. Now that we live in the country and have plenty of space, we compost by simply throwing organic waste onto a large heap (screened from view, of course).

DID YOU KNOW?

Beware of nitrogen robbers

Always layer wood chip and bark mulches on top of your soil—avoid mixing them in. Mulches high in carbon—anything brown—can steal nitrogen from plants. Instead of being there for the plants, soil nitrogen gets used up by microorganisms in the process of breaking the stuff down. Layering high carbon mulches 2" to 4" (5 to 10 cm) deep over the soil is fine. This doesn't take up huge amounts of nitrogen because the mulch breaks down more slowly, with just the upper layer of soil as the site of all the action.

Stuff to Compost

Yes	No
Household waste: fruit and vegetable peelings, egg shells, coffee grounds, loose tea and tea bags **Yard trimmings:** leaves, grass clippings, weeds (before they have seeds), lawn thatch, the remains of garden plants, brush (chopped into small pieces)	Diseased plant material, weeds that have gone to seed, meat, bones, cheese, salad dressing, cooking oil (these foods cause odors and can attract rodents and raccoons)

Much Ado About Mulching

What's this mulch stuff, anyway? Well, it's a blanket of loose material—generally of natural bits and pieces such as chopped up leaves, bark chips, pine needles, straw, or grass clippings—that gardeners put over the soil's surface. Why? Bare soil is not a good thing. Without something growing on it or covering it, topsoil erodes with the wind and rain.

Have you ever noticed how nature quickly covers bare patches of soil with weeds? That's one way of making sure soil stays in place, but gardeners aren't exactly in love with weeds. You can do your part by covering bare soil between plants with a layer of mulch—a job that makes other garden chores easier because, as well as making your beds look neat, mulch does a lot of other neat things. In fact, it's hard to think of another garden job that provides so much payback:

- It keeps weeds down, mainly by blocking out the light they need to germinate—and if a weed does manage to poke through, it's easier to pull it out when it's rooted in a layer of mulch than when it's really anchored in the soil.
- It preserves the soil's moisture by reducing evaporation and helps prevent erosion caused by rain and wind. Bare soil often gets a crust on it that prevents rain from penetrating easily.
- It keeps soil temperatures cooler in summer and helps reduce the risk of damage to plant roots in winter.

 Mulch

Perhaps the strangest mulch I've ever seen was a layer of wine corks spread all over a flower bed. It works just fine (cork is a natural material) if you don't mind your neighbors speculating on your drinking habits. Here are some more conventional choices for mulch:

- **Bark:** Available shredded or in small chips, this material is excellent under trees and shrubs. Avoid the big bark chunks, which aren't as effective.
- **Cocoa bean shells:** Good for flower beds, this one will make the garden smell like yummy chocolate at first, but the aroma fades quickly. This material can get moldy if you lay it on too thick—don't add more than 2" (5 cm)—and it's very light and can blow away. I find that watering well after spreading helps keep it in place.
- **Compost:** Your plants will love it, but unless you have a huge compost pile or can buy it, it's hard to have enough on hand for mulching. When I use compost this way, I use a thin layer and top it with another material such as leaves or straw because compost happens to be a fertile launching pad for weed seeds.
- **Grass clippings:** When fresh, these have high moisture and nitrogen content and can get smelly. The solution? Apply a thin layer. Don't use clippings for mulch when grass is going to seed or it can germinate in your beds and create a grassy weed problem.
- **Fall leaves:** Nature's favorite mulch—great masses of them are free in the fall—they're best if you chop them somehow. Otherwise, they can mat and stop air and water movement into the soil. To chop, use a leaf shredder, drive your lawn mower over them, or put them in a sturdy plastic garbage container and go at them with your weed eater. Use them as winter mulch or save them in bags or in a pile for spring mulching of shrubs and flower beds.
- **Straw:** Keep any bales you buy for autumn decoration because straw makes great mulch for vegetable gardens and is also an excellent winter mulch. With straw, I used to find my biggest weed problem was grain growing from the stray kernels in the bales, but now I store the bales uncovered outdoors over the winter. The bales get wet, causing the grain to germinate in the autumn warmth, then winter cold kills them off. Presto: Come spring, I've got problem-free mulch. The slight spoiling isn't a problem. (Hay is full of seeds, so don't use it as mulch.)
- **Pine needles:** Long-lasting, light, and easy to come by if you have pines—each fall they drop a pile of needles. Leave them in place on top of the soil under your trees or rake them up to use elsewhere in the garden. **Cones** from pines and other evergreens can also be used.

- It helps keep soil from splashing onto leaves, which helps prevent soil-borne fungal diseases and keeps plants looking neater.
- As mulch decomposes, it adds all-important organic matter to the soil and keeps the top layer of soil loose and airy.

The how-to is simple: Just layer the stuff 2" to 4" (5 to 10 cm) deep over bare soil near your plants. Just don't put it right on top of plants, and keep it from touching the bark of trees and shrubs since excess moisture there can cause rot and disease.

Mulch around your plants, not on top of them.

Add mulch to your garden in spring before hot weather comes and while annual and perennial plants are still small enough to work around easily.

Some gardeners add winter mulch to give extra protection to plants—which doesn't keep plants warm but helps keep soil temperatures even—a good idea in areas where winter brings alternating periods of freezing and thawing and where there isn't enough snow cover to give plants a thick blanket of insulation. Boughs cut from your Christmas tree make good winter mulch and have the added bonus of trapping snow that might otherwise blow away.

To Fertilize or Not to Fertilize?

I figure Mother Nature doesn't go around sprinkling granular fertilizer over the landscape and most plants in nature do just fine, so I use very little commercial fertilizer in my perennial garden and my lawn gets only one annual application in late fall. I'm also lucky to garden on rich fertile clay, so for me, the mantra of organic gardening makes sense: Feed the soil and the soil will feed your plants.

As you've already read, if you regularly add enough quality humus and mulch, your soil becomes rich and fertile. And with improved

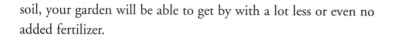

soil, your garden will be able to get by with a lot less or even no added fertilizer.

What's in fertilizer?

All plants need the big three—nitrogen, phosphorous, and potassium, known as NPK for short—as well as secondary nutrients such as sulfur, calcium, and magnesium. Micronutrients—such as iron, manganese, zinc, chlorine, boron, copper, and nickel—are essential too, but in very small quantities. Here's what the big three do:

- **Nitrogen (N)** is the most important factor in plant growth and greening up lawns. Without it, plant growth is stunted, leaving plants looking smaller and paler.
- **Phosphorous (P)** promotes strong root systems and flower and fruit production.
- **Potassium (K)** is important in the process of turning energy from the sun into starches and sugars the plant uses for food.

Fertilizer labels will tell you that a fertilizer is 10-15-10, which means 10% nitrogen, 15% phosphorous, and 10% potassium. So why don't the numbers add up to 100%? The remaining ingredients are fillers. For example, nitrogen is a gas and has to be changed into a stable form, and that requires added ingredients. Also, a mixture containing 100% plant nutrients would be too strong to use.

Plant nutrients are found naturally in healthy, humus-rich soils, but some soils may be low in fertility or lacking in one or more nutrient. For example, nitrogen is soluble and can wash out with rain, so it needs to be continually replaced. One of the most important roles humus plays in the soil is replenishing nitrogen. On new housing sites, soils tend to be both compacted from heavy equipment and depleted of humus and nutrients because the builder has scraped off all the topsoil, leaving new plants to struggle in poor subsoil with only a thin layer of replacement topsoil.

While you're still in the soil improvement phase, using fertilizer will give your plants a boost. Fast-growing, nutrient-gobbling plants such as vegetables also benefit from fertilizer, and plants in containers absolutely depend on it. When using fertilizer products, always follow the instructions on the package: If a little is good, more is not better. Excess fertilizer will burn plant roots and harm soil life forms.

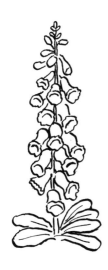

What about organic fertilizer?

People with impressive letters behind their names passionately debate the merits of manufactured chemical fertilizers versus organic ones. Some experts say plants prefer organic sources of nutrients. Equally learned experts argue that the plants don't care: Once a nutrient, say nitrogen, is dissolved in water, it is in its most elemental form and plants can't tell whether it came from manufactured urea or organic blood meal. At the plant root level, a nitrogen molecule is a nitrogen molecule, no matter what its source.

Organic advocates point out that salts in chemical fertilizers harm beneficial soil microorganisms and argue that there are other advantages to using organic sources of nutrients, such as the slow breakdown into nutrient components and sustained feeding. And chemical fertilizers, unlike such fertility-boosting sources of humus as well-rotted manure or compost, do nothing to improve the soil's structure.

One thing is certain: Unless you're using homemade compost or leaf mold to boost your soil's nutrient quotient, you'll find that many organic fertilizers tend to be more expensive than chemical ones.

What about bonemeal?

One widely available organic fertilizer, bonemeal, is falling out of favor as a source of phosphorous. Although some gardeners still swear by bonemeal, experts point out that modern processing methods remove most of the nutrient value and leave today's product inferior to what used to be available.

And now there's an added concern about a potential link to so-called mad cow disease and its human counterpart, variant Creutzfelt-Jakob disease (CJD), which is spread by "prions" from the brains of animals. Prions are infectious, non-living proteins that can't be destroyed by sterilization or burning, which means they survive the rendering process and could end up in products like bonemeal.

While the danger is small, especially in North America—most cases of variant CJD have so far been confined to Britain and Europe—it pays to be cautious. Bonemeal is dusty, and there are concerns that breathing the dust or absorbing it through cuts or bruises could be dangerous. What's more, prions persist in soil for years and years.

Chapter 4

Getting Your Feet Wet: Water-Wise Gardening

Have you ever stood out in the yard on a hot summer afternoon, the sprayer nozzle at the end of your hose in one hand and a tall cool drink in the other, watering the garden? Feels good, doesn't it? The trouble is, you're getting a better drink than your plants are.

What's wrong with this picture? First, you're using the wrong tool for the job. A sprayer nozzle is just the thing for washing the car, but it's practically useless in the garden because it sends out a high-pressure jet that flattens plants, making it almost impossible to deliver water in the quantity needed.

Second, dousing foliage with water doesn't do any good. Your plants may look like they've had a drink, but their roots—the plants' chief means of taking up water—are left high and dry.

If you still don't believe me, water a dry planting bed this way for about 10 minutes, then take a trowel and dig a shallow hole. You'll be surprised to see that the moisture has barely penetrated the soil's top layer.

If you're lucky enough to have an automatic irrigation system, you may never worry about your garden drying out. Just make sure that your system is set up for deep watering once or twice a week and that it can be programmed to skip operating if it's just rained. Overwatering and foliage that's constantly wet can be a big problem with irrigation systems that are timed to water daily.

Plants need water—a healthy plant is 75% to 90% water—and adequate moisture is especially critical during the first few weeks of growth, while plants are building root systems and getting established. It's a great consolation to know that, as with most jobs around the garden, using the right tool at the right time saves effort and resources—yours *and* Mother Nature's. For spot watering individual plants or containers, the better tool is a watering can or a hose-end watering wand (which has a specially designed water breaker with many tiny holes that delivers water in a soft shower rather than a high-pressure stream).

Canada and the United States are the heaviest water users on the planet. We take water for granted because we can: For most of us, it's cheap and readily available. But municipal water usage increases by as much as 50% every summer as a result of watering lawns and gardens—and gardeners don't like to admit it, but a lot of that water is wasted when we splash it around like drunken sailors.

Attitudes are beginning to change as supplies get lower in some of the drier regions and people become more aware of the need to conserve this resource. If you're concerned about water use—and the time you spend watering—follow the tips on efficient watering in this chapter. Then get ready for a welcome treat: a lower water bill, a better garden, and more time for yourself.

Giving Plants What They Need—Without Wasting Water

- Don't water if you don't have to—too much water is as bad as too little. Measure and keep track of rainfall. The ideal for most gardens is an inch (25 mm) every week, but many established plants can easily weather short periods of dryness. If heat and drought are prolonged, water your most valuable plants.
- When you water, give infrequent but generous waterings, about an inch (25 mm) once a week. Avoid frequent shallow waterings, which encourage roots to stay near the soil surface instead of probing more deeply for moisture. The more deeply rooted your plants, the more resilient they'll be in a dry period.

- When you water, moisture should penetrate the top 5" or 6" (12 to 15 cm) of the soil. Dig a small hole with your hand trowel an hour after you've watered to check. Let the soil surface dry between waterings.
- The best time to water is early in the morning or in the evening. In the heat of the day—between 10 a.m. and 6 p.m.—sun and wind quickly evaporate a significant quantity of water.
- Overhead watering with a sprinkler is best done early in the morning so that leaves can dry off through the day. Foliage that's frequently wet overnight creates the perfect environment for fungal diseases.

Deep watering prompts roots to probe farther into the soil for moisture, so your plants weather drought better.

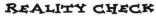 REALITY CHECK

Myth: Water droplets on foliage magnify the sun's rays to cause leaf scorch.

Fact: Not true. This is an old wives' tale that doesn't seem to go away.

The Better Way: Soaker Hoses

When it comes to watering the lawn and the garden, most of us reach for a sprinkler attached to a hose. Various types of sprinklers are readily available and easy to use, but because they throw water into the air, sprinklers can lose an amazing amount of water to evaporation—experts estimate about 50% on a hot, windy afternoon—and even more by errant spraying onto walkways, patios, driveways, and other locales that don't need it.

Sprinklers are better suited to watering lawns than gardens. But for garden beds—whether vegetable, flower, or ground cover plantings—consider soaker hoses. Generally black, they're made of a porous material that looks and feels like a wetsuit, and unlike a regular hose, they're designed to allow water to seep out of tiny holes. They will soak an area about 2' to 3' wide along their whole length, delivering water close to the root zone, where plants will take it up most readily, and not wetting the leaves.

A 100' (30 m) length of soaker hose seeps about half a gallon (2 l) of water per minute, and you can attach several soaker hoses together and snake them through your beds about 3' (1 m) apart to create an effective irrigation system that's amazingly cheap and easy to use. You can leave them in place all season and even through the winter—a

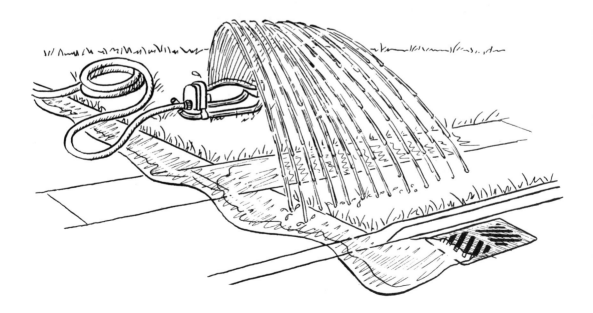

great advantage for permanent plantings such as perennials or ground covers.

I resisted soaker hoses for years. The reason? They need to be set up early in spring, before the plants start growing actively. Invariably, I'd be so busy that I'd leave the job too late. By then, threading the hoses through a jungle of vegetation was about as appealing as wrestling an octopus.

When I finally got my act together and put the soaker hoses in place on time, I couldn't believe the difference—the beds watered by soakers stayed moist much longer than those watered with the sprinkler. And, best of all, the soakers cut down on the amount of hose-hauling and remembering to move the sprinkler head.

Try to have a helper on hand when you're setting up your soaker hoses. They can be stiff at first, but uncoiling them and placing them in the sunshine an hour beforehand helps. Some gardeners bury soaker hoses an inch or two under the ground, or cover them with mulch, but this isn't necessary, as their black coloring makes them virtually disappear, especially when the plants start to grow. (If you bury them, you may slice them with the spade by accident while digging in the garden—yes, I've done it, more than once.)

To use a soaker hose, just attach the regular hose to the end of the soaker and let it run for two to three hours or whatever time the manufacturer recommends. To make the process even simpler, buy a timer that will automatically turn the water on and then off after a certain length of time. Before using, read the manufacturer's instructions: Most soaker hoses operate at a lower water pressure, so your tap needs to be just partly opened.

First Things First: Watering Priorities

You do have a life outside the garden, right? To make this essential task easier, it helps to prioritize by targeting plants that shouldn't dry out during hot, dry periods:

- New plants in their first year, especially new trees and shrubs: Even if these plants are drought-tolerant, they need regular watering until their roots are firmly anchored into the ground. Because trees

Water-efficient plants

Evergreens and broadleaf evergreens	Deciduous shrubs	Deciduous trees	Ornamental grasses	Perennials	Annuals
Colorado spruce (*Picea pungens*)	Bayberry (*Myrica pennsylvanica*)	Amur maple (*Acer ginnala*)	Annual fountain grass (*Pennisetum setaceum*)	Artemisia	Bachelor's buttons (*Centaurea*)
Euonymus	Beautybush (*Kolkwitzia amabilis*)	Bur oak (*Quercus macrocarpa*)	Blue fescue (*Festuca*)	Baby's breath (*Gypsophila*)	California poppy (*Eschscholzia californica*)
Jack Pine (*Pinus banksiana*)	Cutleaf sumac (*Rhus typhina 'Dissecta'*)	Hackberry (*Celtis occidentialis*)	Blue oat grass (*Helictotrichon sempervirens*)	Bearded iris	Cleome
Junipers (*Juniperus*)	Devil's walking stick (*Aralia spinosa*)	Kentucky coffee tree (*Gymnocladus dioicus*)	Fountain grass (*Pennisetum alopecuroides*)	Black-eyed Susan (*Rudbeckia*)	Cosmos
Mugo pine (*Pinus mugo*)	Lilac (*Syringa*)	Crabapple (*Malus*)	'Karl Foerster' feather reed grass (*Calamagrostis x acutiflora 'Karl Foerster'*)	Blazing star (*Liatris*)	Dahlberg daisy (*Thymophylla*)
Red Pine (*Pinus resinosa*)	Mock orange (*Philadelphus*)	Ginkgo		Blanket flower (*Galliardia*)	Four o'clock (*Miribilis jalapa*)
Scotch pine (*Pinus sylvestris*)	Nannyberry (*Viburnum lentago*)	Green ash (*Fraxinus pennsylvanica*)	Little blue stem (*Schizachrium scoparium*)	Catmint (*Nepeta*)	Gazania
Yucca	Potentilla	Honey locust (*Gleditsia*)	Mexican feather grass (*Stipa tennuissima*)	Daylily (*Hemerocallis*)	Geranium (*Pelargonium*)
	Privet (*Ligustrum*)	Ivory silk lilac (*Syringa reticulata 'Ivory Silk'*)	Miscanthus cultivars	Dianthus	Love lies bleeding (*Amaranthus caudatus*)
	Rose of Sharon (*Hybiscus syriacus*)	Red Oak (*Quercus rubra*)	Prairie dropseed (*Sporabolus hetrolepis*)	Lavender (*Lavendula*)	Marigold (*Tagetes*)
	Rugosa roses (*Rosa rugosa*)	Russian olive (*Elaeagnus angustifolia*)	Switchgrass (*Panicum virgatum*)	Peony (*Paeonia*)	Mealycup sage (*Salvia farinacea*)
	Smokebush (*Cotinus coggygria*)			Poppy (*Papaver*)	Portulaca
	Snowberry (*Symphoricapos*)			Salvia	Sunflower (*Helianthus annuus*)
	Spirea			Sea holly (*Eryngium*)	Strawflower (*Helichrysum*)
	Wayfaring viburnum (*Viburnum lantana*)			Sedum	Zinnia
				Snow-in-summer (*Cerastium*)	
				Thyme (*Thymus*)	
				Yarrow (*Achillea*)	

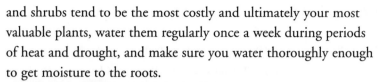

and shrubs tend to be the most costly and ultimately your most valuable plants, water them regularly once a week during periods of heat and drought, and make sure you water thoroughly enough to get moisture to the roots.

- Thirsty perennials: Group moisture-loving plants together in a bed that's easy to water. Perennials such as astilbe, ligularia, and ferns, for example, grow best in moist soil in shade to part shade.
- Annuals and vegetables: These plants do it all in only one season, so they need at least 1" (25 mm) of water a week. Don't let vegetables dry out while the edible part is forming. The most drought-tolerant annuals (see box) need water only the first few weeks after planting out.
- The 1" (25 mm) per week rule goes for lawns too. But if water supplies are limited—or you're fairly laid back—try letting your grass go dormant during summer's hot, dry period as long as no more than four weeks go by without rain or a watering. When temperatures cool and the rain returns, your grass will green up as good as new. (For lawn care, see Chapter 7.)

Help!

My English garden is wilting

Are you tired of spending scorching summers nursing an English-style perennial garden through case after case of the wilts and the shrivels? Maybe it's time to rethink your garden. England is famed for its misty rains and moderate climate, so slaving over an English-style garden where hot, sunny, and parched summers are *de rigueur* suggests a bad case of horticultural denial, don't you think?

Why not try growing plants that can take the heat with less fuss and watering? Look to plants that are at home in the world's drier regions. Many are succulent, with fleshy tissues that act as water reservoirs; others have taproots or grey, fuzzy, waxy, or finely divided leaves. In general, plants with larger leaves need more water.

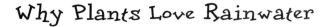

Why Plants Love Rainwater

You can water from the tap all you want, but you've probably noticed that plants look happiest after a good rain. That's because rainwater is often charged with nitrogen from the air, and it's soft and not leaf-chillingly cold.

Well or ground water tends to be hard, containing high levels of calcium or magnesium carbonate, and city water is chlorinated and has added fluoride. None of this is particularly to the liking of plants, although they will put up with it—better a less than perfect drink than no drink at all.

You can collect rainwater from your roof by setting up a rain barrel. A modest rainfall of a quarter of an inch collected from 1,000 square feet of roof yields 150 gallons. (Translated into metric, that's 6 millimeters of water on a 93-square-meter roof netting 680 liters.)

Modern rain barrels, available at many garden stores, come with a shutoff valve and hose connection so you can fill your watering can for easy hand watering. Add a hose extension, and you can let this water dribble into your garden.

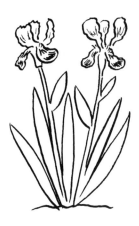

Chapter 5

What's in a Name? Botanical Names in a Nutshell

When I was a new gardener, a friend took me to visit her neighbor—
you know the type: British accent, born with a trowel in her hand.
This intimidating gardener took us on a tour of her perennial border,
pointing out *Monarda didyma* here and *Chelone obliqua* there, and
lord knows what else. I didn't have a clue what she was talking about.

I've learned a thing or two since then, but I'm always struck by
how resistant many gardeners are to botanical names (also called Latin
or scientific names), mostly because of embarrassment about how to
pronounce them. But what earthly use could Latin names possibly be
to the starter gardener? If you're interested in growing perennials and
trees and shrubs, recognizing some botanical names will come in
handy. Really!

For one thing, you're going to stumble across them at the garden
center, in catalogues, and you've already seen them in this book. Most
better nurseries, books, and catalogues organize plants by botanical
name. For another, this naming system is accepted and used the

world over so plant names can be understood whether you speak English, Dutch, or French.

Common names are easy because they're plain English, but they can be confusing because so many plants have more than one common name, or the name is shared by several species. Is the tulip tree in your neighbor's front yard a saucer magnolia or *Liriodendron tulipifera*? Both may be called tulip trees. If you're planting geraniums, do you really mean *Geraniums* or *Pelargoniums*? The latter—popular flowering container plants that aren't hardy in northern regions—are best known by the common name "geranium," but the true geraniums are actually a group of winter-hardy perennials whose common name is "cranesbill."

Last Name First: Genus and Species

Like a person's first and last names, a plant also has a two-part name made up of *genus* and *species*. A genus is like your last name, but with plants the genus comes first (just as your last name comes first in the telephone book). Take the example of Siberian iris, *Iris siberica*: *Iris* is the genus and *siberica* is the species. And notice that the two words are in italics.

Genus tells you a plant is an iris and not a peony; species tells you what sort of iris it is. Besides Siberian, there are bearded, bulbous, dwarf, and many more. Here's a neat trick to help you remember: Think of genus as general, and species as specific. When you see five kinds of irises, it helps to know that they're different, so you can find the one that suits your garden best—for example, bearded irises love to bake in the sun, while Siberian irises thrive in moister, shadier conditions.

So, What's a Cultivar?

This one's easy: the word comes from the words "cultivated variety." People who work with plants select what they think are particularly nice colors, better forms, or a perhaps a different flower shape. These are all attributes that distinguish this particular plant from other plants in the species, and of course, people (being the wordy bunch we are) need to give all this yet another name.

> ### DID YOU KNOW?
>
> Sometimes plant names tell you about the plant, but that's not always guaranteed. Some plants are named using obscure names for a place (*sinensis* means from China or Chinese, for example) or for plant discoverers you've never heard of (*Thunbergii* refers to Carl Peter Thunbergia, a Dutch explorer who introduced many plants to Europe from Japan). But often the species part of the name is quite useful in describing a plant's features, as in the following examples:
> - *alba*: white
> - *aurea, aureo*: golden
> - *fastigiata*: tall, slender, upright, columnar shape
> - *glauca*: blue, describes a blue tint on the leaf
> - *pendula*: weeping growth habit
> - *prostrata*: low to the ground or creeping
> - *purpurea, atropurpurea*: purple
> - *rubra*: red
> - *zebrina, zebrinus*: striped or banded

Remember *Iris siberica*? Well, there are plenty of different Siberian irises to choose from. A gorgeous soft white and butter-yellow one is called *Iris siberica* 'Butter and Sugar.' Two blue-flowered cultivars are the indigo 'Caesar's Brother' and the light blue 'Papillon.' Cultivar names can be one or more words and are always set apart by single quotation marks. For gardeners looking for unique and interesting plants, finding a great new cultivar of a favorite plant is where it's at. Really!

Another term you may stumble on is *variety*, which also refers to a plant that has unique features distinguishing it from the species. The important thing here is that this variation happened *in nature, without human intervention*, whereas cultivars are selected, bred, or propagated by people.

With such plants, you'll notice the short form "var." in the name. For example, an elegant flowering shrub, the doublefile viburnum (*Viburnum plicatum* var. *tomentosum*), differs from the ordinary snowball viburnum (*Viburnum plicatum*) because it has a wealth of gorgeous flat white flowers instead of rounded snowball ones when in bloom.

Attention: Plant Crossing

Plant breeders often create new varieties using the pollen of one plant and the ovule of another, which results in a distinctively new plant referred to as a hybrid. Crosses also happen by accident in nature. Hybridization results in new cultivars and varieties of vegetables, annuals, perennials, and even trees and shrubs.

Sometimes hybrid crosses are designated with an *x*, as in the popular saucer magnolia, *Magnolia* x *soulangiana*, which is a cross between two Chinese magnolias *Magnolia denudata* and *M. lilliiflora* made in the garden of Soulange-Bodin in France early in the 19th century. Now isn't that a neat bit of trivia to amaze your gardening friends?

Help!

How Do I Pronounce Botanical Names?

If you're tongue-tied about pronouncing Latin names, welcome to the club. A good plant book will often help, but just try to sound the name out. Chances are the person you're talking to also has his or her own way of saying it, so write down the name so you can compare it to plant tags or show it to anyone helping you when you're shopping.

To avoid embarrassment, here's the right way to pronounce a popular shrub that's known by its botanical name: *Cotoneaster*. Sounding out doesn't help with this one; it's pronounced *kuh-toh-nee-as-ter*, not *cotton-easter*.

Chapter 6

Bringing Home the Green: When and Where to Buy

One day, as I was getting home from a garden center with yet more plants, my neighbor's seven-year-old daughter said, "Yvonne, do you waste all of your money on plants?"

Ask avid gardeners why they garden, and chances are the answer is a love of plants. Keen gardeners adore plants—they collect them— and are forever on the hunt for the hot plant they haven't yet grown.

Once you start gardening, you'll see plants differently too. First off, you'll actively *notice* them—they won't just be anonymous bits of green and color in the background. And as you learn their names and pick favorites, you too might start scouting around for special plants your neighbors don't have.

When you get the hang of it, they won't be able to keep you out of the garden center, but plant shopping can be nerve-wracking the first time out. When you're just learning to tell a pansy from a petunia, it really *is* a jungle out there—an overwhelming number of plants in way too many colors, shapes, and sizes—and it seems easiest to pick

 Sellers know that customers make a beeline to plants in bloom, but if there's a choice between a plant in full bloom or one that's just beginning to bud, choose the latter so it will bloom in your garden, not the garden store.

the first vaguely familiar thing in bloom and run for the cash register. So let's take the mystery out of plant buying.

Plant sellers run the gamut from small mom-and-pop nurseries to full-service stores with a vast number of plants, along with more tools, gadgets, fertilizers, and soil amendments than you ever thought could exist. These days, plants are even sold in grocery stores, home centers, and superstores. And too often they're left at the mercy of employees who haven't got a clue that plants need regular watering.

Be wary of temporary garden centers that sprout up like crabgrass each spring. They may look like places to grab a bargain, but selection is skimpy and it's a miracle if the plants get watered. And if stock is set up on hot pavement, watch out: A plant that fries for a few days in such conditions can become so badly weakened it may never recover. By midsummer, the temp garden center will be long gone, which isn't a lot of help if your peony poops out. Unless the wares look fresh as a daisy—which tends to be on delivery day—do yourself a favor and stick to real garden centers and nurseries.

Telling a quality garden center from a ho-hum plant seller

Look for:
- Healthy plants with good color and thick (not spindly) stems, in weed-free containers.
- A good selection laid out logically. If you're looking for shade plants, it's a whole lot easier if they are displayed together.
- Labels showing plants in bloom or at mature size, including price, information on how and where to grow, and expected size and spread.
- Aisles wide enough for nursery wagons or carts that hold your purchases.
- Somebody on staff qualified to make planting suggestions and answer horticultural questions. If the guy who's been hired for his muscles doesn't have the answer, ask for the owner.
- Display gardens—showcasing plants growing in real flower beds, not just in pots and cell packs—get bonus points.

How Ornamental Plants Are Sold

Garden plants are sold in a number of ways, most commonly in plastic or fiber containers in a range of sizes. Woody plants, such as trees and shrubs, can also be sold B&B—no, not bed and breakfast, but balled and burlapped—with their roots contained in a burlap-wrapped ball of soil and sometimes wrapped in a wire basket. These plants are field-grown and dug with spading machines, and tend to be larger than container-grown trees and shrubs. Look for:

• Balanced, even growth and well-colored leaves. Avoid yellowed leaves (unless they're supposed to be yellow); browned, stunted, or slimy leaves are signs of insect, wilting, or disease damage.

• Healthy roots. Whether annual, perennial, or woody, if you can do so without damaging the plant—or putting your back out—pop it out of its container and look at the roots. Are they root-bound—hort-speak for a strangled, tangled mass and roots sticking out of the bottom of the pot—or is there a good proportion of soil to roots? Avoid plants with underdeveloped roots. The plant that's been growing in its container for a while is a better buy than the one that was potted up yesterday.

DID YOU KNOW?

Some perennials for sale in spring have been "forced"— coaxed into lush growth and early flowering in green-houses before they would actually bloom in a real garden. The problem? It's easy for new gardeners to get confused about when a perennial actually flowers or to think it'll flower all summer long like an annual. It won't—next season your perennial will bloom at the normal time for the species, which could be mid or even late summer.

Frazzle-free shopping

The busiest time at garden centers is mid spring— around the weekend closest to May 24th or whatever is generally accepted as the frost-free date for your region. To avoid crowds and get the best service, shop at off times: week-days from 9 to 5, early or late in the day, during the dinner hour, or, my favorite, on a cool, rainy day. Just dress for the weather and bring along a pair of garden gloves (or buy them there).

Late summer or early fall can also be a good time to buy and plant perennials and trees and shrubs. Many sellers discount plants so they won't have to overwinter them. These plants may look a little worn, but their leaves are getting ready to die off anyway. Remember, you're buying for next year's growth, so have a look at the roots. If they're strong and healthy-looking, the plant should be fine.

- A neat container. Is the soil surface covered with weeds or moss? Too much of either may be a sign the plant has been growing in its container a long time and may be pot-bound.
- Most annuals are sold in cell packs of four or six plants. So first count them. You'll be amazed how often one plant is stunted or even missing. Good garden centers weed these ones out.

Home, James: Transporting Your Purchases

Plants are alive, and in a parked car on warm days they're as vulnerable as dogs, kids, and ice cream, so get them home and out of the vehicle as soon as possible. If you have a pickup truck, put a tarp over the plants so the wind won't dehydrate them on the road.

It's best to buy plants when you have a garden bed ready for them, but who are we kidding? Most gardeners buy plants when they see something they've got to have. If you're not ready to plant yet, store sun-loving plants where they'll get morning sun and shade lovers in full shade. Check the plants daily, keeping them moist but not sopping wet, but try not to leave them in limbo for more than a week—it's easy to forget to water.

If you're buying a lot of plants or getting larger trees and shrubs, many plant sellers will deliver. They'll even plant trees and shrubs for an extra fee.

Check if your retailer guarantees woody plants for one year after purchase—most do, so hold onto your receipt. But be sure to do your part. Steer clear of problems by buying plants suitable for your conditions—a tree or shrub that loves well-drained soil will languish in a soggy spot. And don't just plant and walk away. If you let a new tree dry out, it won't be the garden center's fault if it dies.

On the other hand, all gardeners have plants die on them. It's not the end of the world, just a good excuse to go plant shopping again.

Buying Plants by Mail Order or On-Line

If you've had a look at garden catalogues (which seem to sprout like crazy in the middle of winter, when gardeners are most vulnerable to their charms) you know you can buy plants sight unseen. Many catalogues are filled with dazzlingly seductive photos—knowing firsthand the plant lust they can inspire, I think of them as "garden porn."

Will the plants look as wonderful in your garden? That depends. Remember, the pictures are intended to sell plants, and some sellers exaggerate big-time. In real life, the plants are almost guaranteed not to look glamorous at first—but, given a season or two, they just might live up to expectations.

Many experienced gardeners shop by mail order for a simple reason: better selection. Few garden centers are big enough to stock a fraction of what's available, so this is a great way to buy what may not be available locally. Many mail order companies concentrate on certain plants. For example, a rose specialist will have hundreds of varieties to offer, while your local garden retailer can afford to bring in only a dozen or so. Some mail order firms specialize in new introductions or rare plants, so you could be the first on your block to grow that Gorgeous Hot New Perennial. Many plant sellers now have Web sites too.

But how to tell who's legit and who's trying to pawn off miserable scraps of greenery to clueless gardeners? First, if the deal is too good to be true, remember the old saw: You get what you pay for. Second, if you read strident headlines promoting sweepstakes, you've got to wonder what they're really selling.

Good mail-order suppliers will tell you:

- Common and botanical names, so you can compare price and shipping size with other suppliers. I've seen unsavory mail-order companies promote ordinary everyday plants available everywhere with colorful names they've made up. Ever heard of a Blue Twinkle?
- Hardiness zone information, so you can tell if a plant can handle your climate.

- Growing requirements—whether the plant is happier in sun or shade or needs special soil conditions—and how big it will get.
- Their returns policy. If you have questions, the seller should be happy to answer them. If you call and they say they can only take orders, hang up.

Think before you leap

Before sending the order:

- Check whether you have a spot for it. You can easily catch spring fever in January and wind up ordering more plants than your garden can hold. Show me a keen gardener who hasn't done that.
- Read the fine print. Check the size of plants shipped. Nothing is more discouraging than paying top dollar for something that comes in a tiny pot. It's happened to me, and I'm supposed to know what I'm doing.
- Keep a record of orders and shipping dates. Could I be the only one who's ever sent for the same tulip bulbs twice after misplacing the original order?

Oh, no, there's no soil!

If your plants come without soil, don't panic. Shipping plants without soil—it's called "bare root"—is a standard practice to keep shipping costs down. As long as the roots were kept moist in damp newspaper

How plants are sold

Bare root

Container-grown

Balled and burlapped

or the like, and you unpack the plants as soon as you get them, this treatment shouldn't hurt your plants. Even if they look dead, stay calm. It may be because they were shipped dormant—hort-speak for the state of limbo when growth shuts down for winter. To reassure yourself, look for buds—that's where you're going to see the first signs of growth.

Your package should come with detailed planting instructions. With bare-root plants, it never hurts to immerse the roots in a bucket of water for an hour or so and then get them planted as soon as possible. A new plant may take some time to leaf out and settle into its new home, so be patient. Don't return it after four days—give it a month or so.

If you feel your mail-order plant is too delicate for the garden or it's still too cold for planting into the garden, try transplanting it into a larger pot and growing it in a sheltered spot for a few weeks. I've done this and find that the plants generally double in size in no time at all.

Chapter 7

Home Turf: Lawns and Lawn Alternatives

Very few outdoor surfaces are as friendly to kids and pets as soft lawn grass. And if you haven't developed a green thumb yet, you'll most likely feel that mowing, though time-consuming, is definitely easier than other garden tasks.

Lawns have been getting a rough ride lately for all sorts of reasons: They guzzle water, and people pour fertilizers and pesticides on them, and then mow them with noisy, polluting machines. It's enough to make you want to kiss your lawn goodbye and skip ahead to the section on ground covers.

But wait a minute. What about a lawn's good points? Like other plants, lawn grasses help to purify water, make oxygen, modify temperatures, prevent erosion, and absorb noise and air pollution.

The really good news is that you can have a lawn without wasting water or using excessive amounts of pesticides and fertilizer. Switch to a reel or an electric mower and you reduce pollution too. Read on for more about sensible mowing, watering, and fertilizing and you'll be on your way to a greener lawn—in both senses of the word—with less effort.

Mow, Mow, Mow Your Lawn

"If I give the lawn a brush cut, I won't have to mow again so soon." Sorry, guys—the care and feeding of lawns still seems to be a guy thing—scalping the living daylights out of the grass leads straight to what you're trying to avoid: more work. Cutting too short weakens your lawn and creates a come-hither zone for insects and weeds. Instead of relaxing in the lawn chair with a cold beer, you'll be fighting weeds and bugs and repairing the grass. Here are some tips for better mowing:

1. **Follow the one-third rule.** Remove only one third of the leaf blade whenever you mow. If you miss a cut, set the mower higher and then cut again at your regular height a few days later.

2. **Mow as soon as the lawn needs it.** There's no hard and fast rule for days between mowing, but mow more often—every five days or so—in spring and fall, when it's cool and wet and the grass is growing like gangbusters, less often in summer, when growth slows down.

3. **Keep your mower's blades sharp.** If the tops of grass blades look yellow or brown after cutting, your mower's blades need sharpening.

4. **Fertilize by leaving clippings on the lawn.** Here's a win-win proposition—less work and saving on fertilizer. Research shows that decomposing clippings provide 25% of a lawn's yearly fertilizer needs. Mulching mowers are designed to chop clippings extra fine, but clippings from a regular mower will quickly disappear if you follow the one-third rule. If you get thick, clumpy clippings, rake them thinner, or collect them for composting or mulching garden beds.

5. **Avoid mowing when the lawn is wet.** Grass clippings will clump up, which can damage the grass under them. Still, it's better to mow when it's damp than to let grass grow too tall.

6. **Vary the pattern and the direction you mow.** Mowing the same old way each time causes soil compaction and wear patterns (not

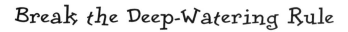

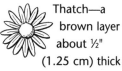
Thatch—a brown layer about ½" (1.25 cm) thick between the soil and green top growth—is an accumulation of dead and decomposing grass stems, leaves, and roots mixed with live roots. If it gets thicker than 1" (2.5 cm), it can be a problem.

The solution? A vigorous raking in late spring and fall, and core aeration at least once a year. Aeration is best done in late spring or early fall, using a machine that removes a core of soil to allow air and water to penetrate into the soil. You can rent the machine or hire a lawn care company to do the job.

to mention boredom). Soil compaction means soil particles get squished together, causing air spaces to shrink. Core aeration is the cure for this. (For more on aeration, see the sidebar to the left.)

7. **Cut your grass one last time in late fall:** Long grass creates the perfect environment for winter fungal diseases, so your last cut of the season should be a little shorter, to 2" (5 cm) in height.

The payback for mowing higher

Mowing recommendations have gone up in recent years—to a height of 3" (9 cm) for Kentucky bluegrass–based lawns, which is most lawns in Canada and the U.S., except in warmer regions of the States. Mow higher and you'll have a better lawn. Here's why:

- Grass is more vigorous because it has more leaf surface to trap sunlight. Leaves make food from sunlight, so if you lop off too much leaf, the plant can't produce and store food. Instead, it uses energy to regrow lost leaves.
- Longer blades shade the grass plants, keeping them cooler and decreasing their need for water. Roots grow more vigorously, which adds drought resistance.
- Lush growth crowds out crabgrass and other low-growing weeds and reduces the light that weed seeds need to sprout.

REALITY CHECK

Myth: Lawns are terrible water guzzlers.
Fact: The average lawn doesn't need any more water than most other landscape plants—1" (25 mm) of water a week, whether from rain or the sprinkler, is enough to keep your grass green, and the grass will stay alive on less. Running the sprinkler for about one to one and a half hours nets about an inch of water. To check, place a couple of empty cans under the sprinkler. When you've collected an inch of water in the cans, you'll have watered enough.

Break the Deep-Watering Rule

The standard advice has been to give lawns one big watering once a week. But new research at Michigan State University has shown that during periods of heat and dryness, frequent light watering—sprinkling 1" inch (25 mm) of water a week but in smaller doses over several days—helps lawns stay green and can prevent some pest and

disease damage to turf. Because lawn grasses have relatively shallow roots, infrequent deep watering doesn't encourage deeper rooting the way it does with other plants.

Give Your Lawn a Boost

Lawns that get fertilizer grow denser and more vigorously and out-compete weeds. When looking at the bag, the three numbers represent the major nutrients in lawn fertilizer—nitrogen, phosphorus, and potassium—in that order.

- Nitrogen makes for healthy green leaves during active growth.
- Phosphorus and potassium are generally not needed in such large amounts, so their numbers are lower.

Let your lawn go brown

Here's a radical idea: Let your lawn to go dormant if the rain goes on strike. "Dormancy" means the grass is taking a midsummer's siesta: It will stop growing and turn a tan color. In return, you get a break from mowing and watering. It's a sensible strategy if there are watering restrictions in your community, don't you think?

I've tried this and it works. We can't do much watering because we rely on a well, so we've let our lawn go brown through three droughts. It's amazing how quickly the grass bounces back to a healthy green a week or so after the weather turns cooler and wetter. Really!

To make this work for you:

- If you've been watering regularly, gradually decrease the amount you give to ease your lawn into dormancy. Stopping all at once stresses the grass too much.
- Dormant lawns can weather five to eight weeks of dryness. If it doesn't rain at all, water monthly, but sparingly, applying ¼" to ½" (6 to 12 mm). The roots will get enough moisture to keep them alive until the rains come back.
- Another benefit of not watering is that lawn grubs have a harder time hatching and surviving in a dormant lawn than in an irrigated one.

Don't spread the stuff by hand or you'll often get patchy and uneven growth. For even distribution, use a fertilizer spreader. You're better off to rent a spreader from a garden supplier or a home center if you don't have one. Most lawn fertilizer bags spell out how much to use and how to adjust your spreader to dole out the right amount.

Never assume that if a little fertilizer is good, a lot more will be better. Too much can burn your grass and run off and pollute water supplies. If fertilizer particles fall on your walkway or driveway, always sweep them back onto the lawn.

If you want to avoid chemical fertilizers, there are many organic ones on the market, but they tend to be more expensive. Alternatively, you can spread an inch or two (2.5 to 5 cm) of compost or well-rotted manure over your lawn in mid spring and early fall instead.

When to fertilize: A new recommendation

Here's how to get one up on your neighbors and have a green lawn more quickly in spring. The latest turf research has shown that fall fertilizer applications are the most important of the year and that you can skip early-spring fertilizing altogether. The thing to do is to give your lawn a *high-nitrogen* fertilizer in late fall as the growth of grass blades is slowing down. The timing will vary depending on where you live—from mid October to Halloween in more northerly regions to late November in warmer regions.

But don't confuse the late-season fertilizer application with fall fertilizers that contain high levels of phosphorus and potassium and low levels of nitrogen. This is the opposite of what research shows turf grasses grown in Canada and the cooler regions of the U.S. prefer.

Why high nitrogen? Since the plants are no longer making top growth late in the fall, they store nutrients from the fertilizer in their roots and crowns, stocking up enough to last into early summer. Another benefit is that fall-fed grass plants suffer less winter dieback and grow vigorous green blades more quickly in spring.

Two extra points to consider:

- If you're aiming for a low-maintenance lawn, this late-fall application is the only one to make. Most quality fertilizers deliver some

nitrogen immediately for fast greening and then release the rest to feed the lawn over a period of weeks. For the late-fall application, look for fertilizer in which nitrogen is listed on the bag as sulfur-coated urea, or isobutylidene diurea (IBDU).

- Aside from the all-important late-fall application, lawns can benefit from fertilizer in early summer, but don't fertilize them in the heat of July and August. Some experts recommend making another application in early fall to help grass recover from the summer's stress.

Feeding and weeding: A word of caution

Products that kill weeds and fertilize the lawn at the same time are popular, as they promise to meet two goals with half the work. If you use them, however, you're spreading a big dose of herbicide over an entire lawn, whether it's really weedy or not.

There's growing concern about the safety of herbicides, particularly where children and pets play on the grass. And if the particles get spread onto other planting areas by mistake, they can damage your tomatoes or your favorite flowers.

If you've got just a few weeds and a small lawn, try hand weeding instead. A weeding knife lets you pry weeds like dandelions and plantain out quite easily. If you have to use herbicides, a better way is to spot spray individual weeds with a small amount of the appropriate product and to fertilize your lawn separately. To avoid exposure to active ingredients of the weed killer, follow product instructions, and keep pets and children away until sprayed areas have dried. By the way, lawn weed herbicides are more effective when used in the fall than in spring.

If the weeds have won out—your lawn is more than half weeds—you're better off to renovate it by killing the old turf and the weeds, and then resod or reseed.

Starting a Lawn from Scratch

Don't just think of a lawn as the best way to fill up your yard. Instead of grassing the entire space, you're better off to plan the shape of your lawn—whether square, rectangular, curved, or round—and then arrange other plants—trees, shrubs, perennials, and annuals—in beds around it.

In spots where grass is going to create headaches, substitute ground covers (which are covered starting on page 64). Ground cover plants are a terrific way to trim mowing chores and get rid of the following problems:

- Having to trim grass under or beside a fence
- Mowing where low tree and shrub branches threaten to grab you
- Slopes that are an athletic feat to cut
- Areas of dense shade where grass poops out instead of growing and tree roots trip you up
- Regions where the climate isn't suitable for grass

Never roll your lawn

Ever noticed old-timers getting out their lawn rollers every spring? The trouble is that rolling doesn't do a thing for rises and dips in the lawn. Adding extra soil or compost and patching with sod or new grass seed is the best way to solve that particular problem. Rolling just leads to soil compaction (squeezing the all-important air spaces out of the soil) and can damage grass roots.

In fact, rolling is called for only after laying sod to ensure good contact of the roots and the soil or when you're pressing grass seed into the soil after sowing a new lawn. So don't copy the old-timers—an unrolled lawn is healthier.

Sod it or seed it?

Most new lawns today are laid with purchased sod. It's more expensive, but you get instant lawn. All you have to do is keep it well watered until it roots into the soil, which will take about four to six weeks. The best time to get seed or sod established is in late summer to early fall, and the second best time is in spring.

To grow a healthy lawn from sod—or seed, for that matter—till the soil and enrich it if necessary (see Chapter 3) and rake it smooth. Lawn needs at least 4" (10 cm) of topsoil to thrive.

Overseeding your lawn

More homeowners should know one of the trade secrets of professional turf managers. If you're serious about a lush, thick lawn, it's an excellent idea to overseed it either in spring or fall with quality grass seed. The new grass seed will grow in thin or bare spots where you've killed weeds or the lawn has died back. The thicker your lawn, the healthier it will be and the fewer weed problems, leading to less use of weed killers—it's a win-win proposition all around.

HOW TO OVERSEED

- Mow the existing lawn extra short—to a height of 1½" (3.5 cm).
- Rake to remove clippings and loosen thatch and soil. Remove all debris so lawn seed can make direct contact with soil.
- Spread seed by applying half of it in one direction at the recommended spreader or broadcast rate; then apply the rest, going over the same area in the other direction. (This makes for even application of seed.)
- Rake seed into the soil by raking in two directions.
- Keep the soil moist with frequent light watering until the new grass seed is established, which will take about four to six weeks.

Grass seed: Know what you're buying

All grass seed may look alike, but you get what you pay for. Unfortunately, seed companies don't have to list the contents of their grass seed mixtures. To find a good bag of seed, you may have to spend time studying the fine print on half a dozen seed bags, as I do every time I buy the stuff. Here's what you should know:

- Be picky. Buy only seed that lists the ingredients. If the grass species aren't listed, it's a tipoff of a low-quality mix likely to contain a lot of *annual* as opposed to *perennial* ryegrass. (If the label just says "ryegrass," chances are it's annual.) Annual ryegrass sprouts quickly but is coarse and lasts only one season. Better grasses such as Kentucky bluegrass take up to three weeks to

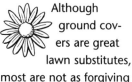 Although ground covers are great lawn substitutes, most are not as forgiving for walking on—but you can put a path of stepping stones through them.

germinate and a couple of months to grow into a thick green carpet.

- A good all-purpose seed mix contains about 40% Kentucky bluegrass and 20% perennial ryegrass, with the rest made up of one or two types of fescue.
- If you want a tough, low-maintenance lawn for sun or shade, choose a mixture with a high percentage of red and/or chewings fescue. Fescues are shade-tolerant and get by with less water and fertilizer than other grass species.

Lawn Alternatives: A Case for Ground Covers

Perennial ground cover plants are a neat solution to many a garden challenge. Think of them as a lushly growing carpet that replaces lawn on tricky spots like slopes or under trees where grass often sulks—as does the poor soul who has to mow there.

A sunny meadow can also make a good substitute for a labor-intensive lawn or flower border, but getting one started is more involved than shaking a can of wildflower seeds over the grass. You'll find more about meadow gardens at the end of this chapter.

The garden's supporting cast

Getting ground cover plants established takes a little effort and patience, but the good news is once they're growing well, they will be much less work than a lawn that has to be mowed week after week. A thriving patch of ground cover is virtually guaranteed to leave very little elbow room for weeds—any plant that does that is a winner in my book.

Plants classed as ground covers are normally low, spreading perennials or woody plants that make thick growth. They can be used to tie a group of shrubs together in a unified bed; under trees, they ensure that you or your sweetie keeps the string trimmer away from vulnerable tree bark.

Ground cover basics

When planning an area of ground covers, keep in mind:

1. **Plant in the right spot the first time.** Like trees and shrubs, ground cover plantings are pretty permanent. It's tough to expel a mass of well-rooted ivy or pachysandra, so pick your spots carefully and make sure the plants are adapted to your soil and your patterns of sun and shade.

2. **Mix and match.** Ground cover plantings don't need to be all of one type. Try a lower-growing mat of ground cover out of which taller perennials grow (the hort term is "underplanting"). For example, I've underplanted the huge hosta cultivar 'Krossa Regal' with a carpet of sweet woodruff. The plants complement each other—the large blue leaves of the hosta contrast nicely with the finer-textured foliage of the sweet woodruff.

3. **Decide when to plant.** Spring planting has its advantages—the plants have a longer growing season to get established before it gets cold. Early fall is also a good time as long as plants have six to eight weeks to get rooted in before freeze-up.

4. **Do your soil homework.** First, get rid of any perennial grasses and weeds and their underground roots and stems, and then turn the soil. (See "Making Your Bed," page 29). If you're working in a spot that's thick with tree roots, you won't be able to work the soil deeply, if at all, so try to add a 2" (5 cm) layer of humus and mix it into the top layer as well as you can (if you can't work it in at all, layer it on top). Just remember: Dumping a thick layer of new soil

Mulch before planting

It's easy to prevent the crowns of small, relatively closely spaced plants from being buried by the mulch when you know this useful landscapers' trick. Just spread a layer of mulch about 2" (5 cm) thick over the planting area. To plant, use your gloved hands or a rake to sweep a patch of mulch aside, put in the plant—setting individual plants no deeper than they were in the flat or pot—and then smooth mulch around it, keeping the crown free of the stuff. When you're finished planting, presto, so is the mulching.

over existing tree roots is a no-no, however, as you can damage trees by suffocating the roots. A thin layer of soil or compost is acceptable—6" (15 cm) is not.

5. **Give it time.** It will take two or three seasons for your plants to grow into a weed-suppressing carpet. (See ground cover lists below for recommended spacing.) In the meantime, a 2" (5 cm) layer of mulch such as shredded bark, wood chips, or cocoa bean hulls will help keep the soil moist and weeds down. Water plants regularly in the first couple of seasons—1" (25 mm) of water weekly, especially during dry periods. The shade under trees such as maples tends to be dry and ground covers planted there will need extra watering even after they are established.

6. **Check regularly for weeds.** Pull them out whenever you see them. Remember, once your ground cover is established, it will be less work than a lawn. Really!

A dozen great ground covers for your garden

The "big three" ground covers are pachysandra, vinca (periwinkle), and ivy, but there are dozens of other options. Here's a sampling of popular choices for sun and shade.

FOR SUN

(Where indicated, some of these are also shade-tolerant.)

- **Bearberry cotoneaster (*Cotoneaster dammeri*):** Low-growing shrub, hardy from zones 4 to 8. Evergreen but loses foliage in colder regions. Glossy leaves, tiny white flowers in late spring. 'Skogholm' produces glossy red berries, 'Coral Beauty' coral berries. Excellent for banks and slopes. Grows 12" (30 cm) tall. Space: 3' to 5' (1 to 1.5 m) apart.

- **Creeping juniper (*Juniperus species*):** Low-growing evergreen shore juniper (*Juniperus conferta*) cultivars 'Emerald Sea' and 'Blue Pacific' are hardy from zones 5 to 9, salt-tolerant, and grow 8" to 12" (20 to 30 cm) tall. Space: 5' to 10' (1.5 to 3 m) apart. Creeping juniper (*Juniperus horizontalis*) cultivars are hardy from zones 3 to 9. 'Bar Harbor,' 'Blue Chip,' 'Emerald Spreader,' 'Prince of Wales,' 'Turquoise Spreader,' and 'Wiltonii' (also called 'Blue Rug') are all excellent. Space: 3' to 5' (1 to 1.5 m) apart.

- **Cutleaf stephanandra (*Stephanandra incisa 'Crispa'*):** Low, wide-spreading deciduous shrub with arching branches, hardy from zones 3 to 7. Flowers aren't showy. Tends to root wherever stems touch soil, great on slopes, and tolerates light shade. Grows 18" to 36" (46 to 90 cm) tall. Space: 3' to 5' (1 to 1.5 m) apart.
- **Fragrant sumac (*Rhus aromatica 'Gro-low'*):** Low, spreading deciduous shrub, hardy from zones 3 to 9. Glossy foliage, fast-growing, and excellent for slopes. Red fruit in late summer. Salt- and shade-tolerant. Grows 2' (60 cm) tall and spreads 6' to 8' (1.8 to 2.5 m). Space: 3' to 4' (1 to 1.2 m) apart.
- **Lilyturf (*Liriope muscari*):** Perennial, hardy from zones 6 to 9. Evergreen in the southern U.S., where it's very popular. Blue, purple, or lilac flower spikes and strap-like leaves. Foliage solid green or variegated in yellow or white. Shade-tolerant. Grows 9" to 12" (22 to 30 cm) tall. Space: 8" to 12" (20 to 30 cm) apart.
- **Thyme (*Thymus* species):** Herb, hardy from zones 4 to 10, depending on cultivar. Small green, grey-green, or golden leaves, with rosy-pink or lilac flowers; creeping growth habit; excellent for well-drained areas; will tolerate some foot traffic. Forms low-growing mats. Space: 12" (30 cm) apart.

FOR SHADE

- **English ivy (*Hedera helix*):** Evergreen ground cover or climbing vine for sun or shade, hardy from zones 4 to 9. Does not flower or fruit until very old. Many cultivars are killed at temperatures below −10°F (−23°C); hardier ones include 'Baltica,' 'Thorndale,' and 'Wilson.' Pruning is necessary to keep it within limits; some species grow rampantly in warmer areas. Try not to let it climb trees. Height: 1' (30 cm) when grown as ground cover, but spreads indefinitely and has clinging rootlike holdfasts that allow it to climb walls to a height of 90' (27 m). Space: 18" (46 cm) apart.
- **Heartleaf brunnera, or Siberian bugloss (*Brunnera macrophylla*):** Perennial, hardy from zones 3 to 7, with large, heart-shaped leaves and small blue flowers in spring. Grows 12" to 18" (30 to 46 cm) tall. Space: 18" (46 cm) apart.
- **Pachysandra (*Pachysandra terminalis*):** Evergreen ground cover, hardy from zones 3 to 8. Grows 6" to 10" (15 to 25 cm) tall. Space: 10" (25 cm) apart.

- **Periwinkle (*Vinca minor*):** Dark green, vining, evergreen ground cover with dainty blue flowers, hardy from zones 3 to 8. Grows about 6" (15 cm) tall. Space: 18" (46 cm) apart.
- **Sweet woodruff (*Galium odoratum*):** Perennial, hardy from zones 4 to 7. White flowers in spring and attractive whorled leaves that die back in winter. Grows 6" to 12" (15 to 30 cm) tall. Space: 12" (30 cm) apart.
- **Wintergreen (*Gaultheria procumbens*):** Native North American woody perennial, hardy from zones 3 to 7. White, bell-shaped flowers in mid spring, followed by scarlet berries, with lustrous, creeping evergreen foliage that's fragrant and turns bronze in the fall. Prefers moist, acid soil (if moss grows in your area, wintergreen will do well) and makes a good underplanting for rhododendrons and other acid-loving plants. Grows 6" (15 cm) tall. Space: 12" (30 cm) apart.

(For more ground cover ideas for shade, see Chapter 9.)

Another Kind of Ground Cover: A Prairie

"Prairie" is the French word for meadow, which is simply a plant community of flowering perennials and grasses growing together. Prairie landscapes are natural to midwestern regions of North America, but today very little original prairie remains. Restoration projects are underway in many regions, and many adventurous gardeners are replacing lawns with prairie-style meadows. It's quite a jump from the manicured lawn, and sometimes the neighbors do raise their eyebrows a tad, but the idea is growing in popularity. One way to keep the neighbors happy is to keep a trimmed border of lawn around your meadow.

Let's assume you're interested in planting a small meadow in an average-sized yard to replace a strip of lawn or a flower bed. It's easier to use container-grown transplants, which bloom much sooner than a meadow from seed. (Seed is cheaper for larger projects, but some of the plants take about three seasons to reach blooming size.)

Step-by-step guide for a backyard meadow

1. Start with a clean, weed-free planting area in a sunny spot. Turn the soil with a spade and fork or a tiller. Rake smooth.
2. Plant in spring to give root systems plenty of time to establish, spacing plants about 12" (30 cm) apart. Water well.
3. Mulch with 3" to 4" (7 to 10 cm) of clean straw to help keep the soil moist and prevent weeds from germinating.
4. Water until transplants are established, especially if there isn't enough rain.
5. Weed carefully in the first growing season (once plants are established, they'll shade out most weeds).
6. Cut plants back in early spring and remove cut material to expose soil to the sun to help warm it.

What to plant

As befits plants that evolved in regions where winters are long and cold, and summers hot and dry, what you'll find listed here are tough beauties that attract butterflies and seed-eating songbirds. In most cases, you don't need to fuss with the soil or add fertilizer—all they need is a sunny spot in average soil. Aside from spacing them about 1' (30 cm) apart, you don't need to worry about height or spread either, as these perennials will grow as a plant community. Unlike carefully grouped perennials in a traditional bed, here you simply plant randomly. Think of it as free-form gardening.

FLOWERING PLANTS

- **Black-eyed Susan (*Rudbeckia hirta*):** Yellow flowers from mid-summer to early fall.
- **Butterfly weed (*Asclepias tuberosa*):** Orange flowers in mid-summer.
- **Heath aster (*Aster ericoides*):** Tiny white flowers in late summer to early fall.
- **Lanceleaf Coreopsis (*Coreopsis lanceolata*):** yellow flowers in mid-summer.
- **Lavender hyssop (*Agastache foeniculum*):** Purple flowers in mid to late summer.
- **Prairie dock (*Silphium terbinthinaecum*):** Large, showy leaves; yellow flowers in mid-summer.
- **Prairie smoke (*Geum triflorum*):** Pinkish flowers in spring, followed by feathery seed heads.
- **Purple coneflower (*Echinacea purpurea*):** Mauve-pink flowers from mid summer to early fall.
- **Shooting star (*Dodecatheon meadia*):** White, pink, or purple flowers in spring.
- **Smooth penstemon (*Penstemon digitalis*):** White flowers in early summer.
- **Wild bergamot, or bee balm (*Monarda fistula*):** Lavender flowers from midsummer to early fall.
- **Prairie dock (*Silphium terbinthinaecum*):** Large, showy leaves; yellow flowers in mid-summer.

GRASSES

In nature, meadows tend to be dominated by grasses, and short to medium-sized North American grasses are wonderful companions for meadow perennials. For a more colorful meadow, use 40% grasses and 60% flowers; for a grassier look, half to two thirds of the plants should be grasses like these:

- **Little blue stem (*Schizachyrium scoparium*):** Medium-sized blue-green clumping grass; flowers and turns coppery in fall.
- **Prairie dropseed (*Sporobulus heterolepis*):** Attractive fine-textured, fountain-like green hummock; leaves turn bronze in fall; fall-blooming flowers have a scent like cilantro.
- **Side oats gramma (*Bouteloua crutipendula*):** Short green clump with attractive oat-like seed heads on one side of the stem.

Chapter 8

Color Your World: Planting a Flower Garden

At last! Flowers are probably what aroused your interest in gardening in the first place. A gorgeous flower garden is an artfully seductive piece of work—but unlike a painting that's actually finished when the artist packs the brushes away, gardens have an incredible habit of changing over time.

Consider the transformation that a single perennial goes through from early spring, when it re-emerges from the ground, to flowering, going to seed, and then dying back in autumn—and remember that most perennials get bigger year by year and that the odd one will just disappear. Responding to inevitable change is precisely where the challenge comes in. Nobody creates a prize-winning flower garden the first year—but you weren't going to invite the garden club over for coffee just yet anyway, were you?

Follow the general principles set out in this chapter, and you'll learn how to create flower beds that look like a garden and not just a random collection of plants that somehow landed in your yard. There

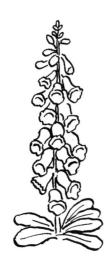

are countless choices—some purely aesthetic, some purely horticul-tural—but the more closely you base your decisions on meeting the growing requirements of your plants (the horticultural stuff of light, soil, moisture levels, and so on) *and* on what looks good to you, the more likely you are to succeed.

When you're starting out, it's easy to think that all you have to do is plant perennials, and with the exception of weeding, watering, and cutting back, your garden is done. Here's what really happens: In the first year, your new plants are underwhelming—the clumps small, the flowers sparse. By the second year, they've grown fuller and have more flowers—but in the third season, watch out. Your plants look like they're on steroids and you look like an accomplished gardener.

But your perennials keep growing—some so aggressively that they crowd out their neighbors with spreading habits that are too much for your garden. Then there are plants that go into an inexplicable decline, and others you decide aren't the right color or aren't quite what you expected.

The solution? The vigorous plants that you like you divide and move to other garden beds or give away (what are friends for?). The ailing ones you try in a new spot that you hope suits them better. And the aggressive ones and those you don't really like you boot out (try the compost pile).

Then you start adding plants and moving others around to fill gaps or to create better-looking or more compatible plant combinations, or...well, you get the point. I did this so much when I started out that my husband said my perennials should have been on wheels.

All this activity adds up to—you guessed it—*gardening*. Veteran gardeners are quick to tell you that no garden is ever truly finished. (But it does get better. I don't move my perennials nearly as much as I used to do.)

Before getting started, ask yourself:

- **What style do I like best?** Do you prefer straight lines or curves? Casual flowers tumbling over each other or a more formal look? Your house may provide a starting point. For example, symmetri-cal, formal designs often suit traditional homes, while a house with gingerbread trim looks romantic surrounded by a colorful profu-sion of flowers. A contemporary home may call for a hint of restraint, say in the style of a Japanese garden or bold plants in large groups.

- **How much space do I have?** Beginners tend to make their beds too narrow because they're intimidated by the task of filling them. (Believe me, that'll be the least of your problems—plants grow, and soon you'll be moaning about the ones you don't have space for.) Aim for a bed that can accommodate three layers—front, middle, and back. Anything narrower than 5' feet (1.5 meters) won't allow for the layering that gives the lush look you're aiming for. I prefer beds that are even wider—at least 6' to 10' (1.8 to 3 meters).

- **Island bed or border?** As the name implies, island beds are islands of flowers planted in a sea of grass. They can look wonderful with taller plants in the middle and others arranged so they'll look good from all sides—or they can resemble blobs of color washed up on the lawn. When they don't look great, it's usually because they're out of proportion (too small for a big yard) or set smack dab in the middle of an otherwise empty yard. A big yard can look good with a series of island beds, but you're better off not to break up a small yard with an island. A flower border, on the other hand, is usually set against a backdrop, which might be the fence between you and your neighbor, the wall of a house or garage, a hedge, or the edge of a patio.

- **What's my season?** Do you want a garden that's colorful all season long or just in certain periods? If you routinely go away in mid-summer, for example, consider a garden that bursts with color from spring bulbs, early perennials, and flowering shrubs but is low-maintenance in midsummer. It can have another peak of

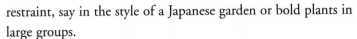

Remember that flowers face into the sun.

A friend of mine wasn't pleased to discover that the clematis vines she'd planted at her south-facing trellis were blooming on her neighbor's side of the fence. A better spot for them would have been on the east-facing fence, where bright afternoon sunshine from the southwest would have coaxed the flowers to show their faces on the "right" side of the fence.

Help!

I don't have much sun

For gardens that hover between sun and shade, there are many plants that thrive in less light. Some favorites include Siberian iris, cranesbills (the hardy perennial geraniums), hostas, and coral bells.

bloom in late summer, and some shrubs and trees that give fall color. If you only have time after work, think evening-scented plants, light-coloured flowers, and garden lighting.

- **How much sun does my garden get?** If your garden doesn't get more than a couple of hours of direct sunlight a day or basks in dappled shade most of the time, choose plants that can take shade or part-shade conditions. (For more on shade gardening, see Chapter 9.) Most flowering plants love full sun, which means they need at least six hours of direct sunlight a day. Many yards have areas of both sun and shade, so keep that in mind when you're choosing plants.

Your Paint Box: The Plants

Okay, you're the artist, your yard is the canvas, and the plants are your colors. Your primary paints include perennials, annuals, biennials, bulbs, vines, and ornamental grasses. Read on for details on each.

Never underestimate the power of a good line

What every flower garden needs to set it apart is a sense of definition. Forget wiggly curves. A smooth, sweeping curve or a clean, straight line will always make a more elegant statement than a wavy pattern twisting all over the yard.

An easy way to visualize the edge of a planting bed is to use a garden hose for curves or a string line for straight lines. As you try out different lines, you should get to the one that feels right. Look from a distance and from inside the house, and if it's still pleasing, eureka, you've got it.

Perennials

Perennials are the backbone of the flower garden because they have staying power. The charm of a garden dominated by perennials is the fact that it changes month by month, constantly giving you new flowers to appreciate as spring moves into fall. The leaves of most perennials die back as winter approaches, but with luck, in spring, they come back into leaf and then into flower. Some perennials are short-lived, but old favorites like daylilies, hostas, and peonies can last for decades.

Unlike most annuals, which bloom their hearts out all season, most perennials flower for only two to four weeks each summer. To create a satisfying garden, choose perennials that bloom at different times so there's always something in flower from early spring through summer and into fall. We'll get to the nuts and bolts of that in a bit.

Annuals

Annuals are the plant world's equivalent of a summer romance. "Live fast and die young" applies here, as true annuals go through their life cycle—growing, flowering, setting seed, and dying—in one season. Some plants most of us consider annuals are actually perennials in warmer climates, for example, geraniums (*Pelargonium* species.)

Modern annuals are bred for constant color through the season and make great supporting players in the flower garden. Annuals that mix beautifully with perennials include spider flower (*Cleome*), cosmos, blue salvia, Brazilian verbena, sweet alyssum, annual fountain grass (*Pennisetum*), marguerite daisies, and love-in-a-mist (*Nigella*).

They're also indispensable space fillers in the first seasons while you're waiting for the perennials to bulk up.

Biennials

Often sold in the perennials section, these plants grow leaves in the first season, come into flower in the second, and then, like annuals, go to seed and die off (though they often self-seed in the garden).

"Why bother?" you may ask. Well, some of these plants are so stunning—foxgloves, verbascums (mulleins), and hollyhocks, for example—that you'll covet them.

Flower bulbs

Actually, "bulb" is an umbrella term for plants that be can be derived from bulbs, corms, or tubers, but for most gardeners, the distinctions aren't terribly important. What they all have in common is swollen underground storage organs that reserve energy for the next season's growth and flowering.

Snowdrops, crocuses, tulips, and daffodils are the familiar bulbs synonymous with spring—nothing tops them for early-season color. There is also a class of summer bulbs—gladioli, dahlias, begonias, and calla and canna lilies—that are perennial, but they won't survive outdoors in colder climates unless dug up and stored in a frost-free place.

Vines

If you have trellises or supports for them to clamber over, vines are a great addition to the flower garden. A favorite perennial climber is the genus *Clematis,* with many varieties boasting stunning flowers. Annual vines such as morning glory, sweet peas, and—my favorite—hyacinth bean, which has purple flowers followed by purple pods, are easy to grow and will fill out your trellis until perennial vines get established. (For more on vines, see Chapter 10.)

Ornamental grasses

The airy appeal of grasses comes from their form, their texture, and their movement with the slightest breeze. Another plus is that they provide interest all season long: In summer, their foliage is lovely, then in autumn they flower and change color. And don't be in a rush to cut them down in late fall—their straw-colored foliage can provide garden interest all winter long. Many annual and perennial varieties are available. Here are some well-behaved, clump-forming perennial types:

- **Hakone grass (*Hakonechloa macra* 'Aureola'):** Yellow and green striped leaves; stems arch gracefully to one side. Hardy to zone 5; shade. Height/spread: 24" to 36" inches (60 to 90 cm).
- **'Karl Foerster' feather reed grass (*Calamagrostis* x *acutiflora* 'Karl Foerster'):** Upright, clump-forming, attractive wheat-like flowers in early summer. Hardy to zone 4; full sun. Height/spread: 4' (1.2 m).
- **Morning light miscanthus (*Miscanthus sinensis* 'Morning Light'):** Clumping grass, narrow leaves with green and white variegation; graceful vase form. Hardy to zone 5; full sun. Height/spread: 4' (1.2 m).

Arranging Flowers in Your Garden

So you've decided where your bed will go and how wide it should be, you have a rough idea of flowers you'd like to include, and you have a vision of how you'd like your garden to look...well, you will one day.

But how do you start? Aren't there some rules you can follow? Well, yes, there are, and once you're a little more comfortable with the business of growing things, you can break some of them if you want. After all, the person you're trying to please is yourself.

Choosing and mixing your colors

What's your color scheme? Do you like hot colours? Can't abide orange? Love pastels? Or do you prefer a restful foliage garden with just a few spots of color? Color is intensely personal, so let your preferences lead you.

Here are some time-tested ways to use color. You could restrict yourself to one approach—a wise move if your garden is small—or if you have more space, try different effects in different parts of the garden.

- For a subtle effect, stick to cooler pastel shades—mauve, pink, white, and shades of blue. This is particularly effective in small gardens.

- Use contrasting colors for bold, eye-catching effects—blue and yellow, orange and purple, red and white. You won't want to do this over the entire garden—too much contrast can go over the top—but contrasting colors here and there add spark.
- Have the best of both worlds—the subtle and the bold—by varying your color scheme with the season. For example, spring and early summer might be all in pastels—tulips in white and pink along with pale yellow and white daffodils, leading to pink peonies paired with Siberian irises blooming in mauve and blue. Then, come the heat of summer, the color scheme switches to a bolder palette with tawny orange and mahogany heleniums, pink echinaceas with their bold copper centers, and chrome yellow black-eyed Susans. Because the bloom times of these perennials are different, you won't create color clashes.
- If a color clashes, pick the problem flower and walk it around the garden, holding it up to the other flowers to see if you can find a better match.
- Single-color gardens have the undeniable appeal of sophistication. I've seen spectacular examples of borders planted all in red or white or yellow. Besides discipline, the secret to success with monochromatic schemes is using the particular color you've chosen in its varying shades, from pale and pastel to dark and rich, and playing leaf textures and colors off against each other as well.

Terrific perennials for every purpose

Edgers	Fillers for the middle	Backdrop plants
Daylilies (*Hemerocallis*)	Butterfly gaura (*Gaura lindheimeri* 'Whirling Butterflies')	Autumn sun rudbeckia (*Rudbeckia nitida* 'Herbstsonne')
Catmint (*Nepeta* x 'Dropmore Blue')	Globe thistle (*Echinops ritro*)	Goat's beard (*Aruncus dioicus*)
Lady's mantle (*Alchemilla mollis*)	Peony (many cultivars available)	Joe Pye weed (*Eupatorium cultivars*)
Thread-leaved coreopsis (*Coreopsis verticillata* 'Moonbeam,' 'Zabgreb,' and 'Golden Shower')	Russian sage (*Perovskia atriplicifolia*)	Monkshood (*Aconitum cultivars*)
Carpathian bellflower (*Campanula carpatica* 'Blue Clips' and 'White Clips')	Coneflower (*Echinacea purpurea* 'Magnus' or 'White Swan')	Wild blue indigo (*Baptisia australis*)

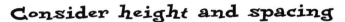

Consider height and spacing

Check how tall and wide your plants are supposed to get—the plant tag should say—and think of them in terms of edgers (front of bed), fillers (middle of bed), and backdrop.

Plant taller annuals and perennials toward the back of your beds, but break this rule occasionally to avoid the high-school-bleacher syndrome. Let a taller group rove into the middle and a mid-high group nudge into the front. Try putting some tall plants that are airy and see-through near the front, which works beautifully with ornamental grasses or Brazilian verbena.

How far apart should you plant? About as far as the plant's ultimate spread—a perennial that grows 24" (60 cm) wide should be about 20" to 24" (50 to 60 cm) from its neighbors. Ornamental grasses I place as far apart as their final height because I don't want their form to be spoiled by overcrowding. (I actually use a tape measure, as I tend to plant too closely).

Mixing it all up

The trend nowadays is not to segregate flowers in their own garden, but to plant what is called a "mixed border" in which small flowering trees and shrubs join the flowers to flow into a pleasing arrangement that looks good all season long—yet another reason not to stint on the width of your beds.

The bulbs are the season-openers, the annual and perennial flowers star during the warmer months, and deciduous shrubs make their own contributions—some with flowers, others with attractive stems, leaves or berries, or fall color—while evergreens provide a touch of green to keep things interesting in the off-season. A few pointers:

- This style is practical for today's smaller properties, which don't have enough space for separate beds of shrubs and flowers.
- A garden populated with one of this and one of that tends to look jumbled and in need of something to pull it all together. Most experts recommend planting all except some of the largest stand-alone plants in odd-numbered groups of three, five, seven, or more. But you'll notice that gardeners—especially those with a huge appetite for plants and small spaces—break this rule all the time.
- Imaginative gardeners try to create unity in other ways. For example, they may limit their colors to two or three that harmonize well, or put some plants into groups of three and repeat them among single specimens of other plants. They might rely on a strong backdrop, such as an evergreen hedge, or use one type of plant as the edger along the front of the bed. You get the picture.

 Small trees and shrubs

Small flowering trees and shrubs and evergreen shrubs that mix well with annuals and perennials include:
- shrub roses (*Rosa*)
- star magnolia (*Magnolia stellata*)
- dogwood (*Cornus*)
- dwarf crabapple (*Malus*)
- serviceberry (*Amelanchier*)
- hydrangea
- purple smoke bush (*Cotinus coggygria*)
- boxwood (*Buxus*)
- dwarf yews (*Taxus*)
- upright and creeping junipers (*Juniperus*)

Aim for continuous bloom

This is the business that makes flower gardening such a challenge for beginners and experts alike. Many annuals bloom all summer, but most perennials bloom for a specific time only, usually a week or two, maybe even a month if it's a longer-blooming plant. The trick is to group plants so that as one clump is fading, nearby plants are coming into flower.

New gardeners often get into trouble by shopping only in spring and buying what's in bloom then. By July, their garden is finished. To solve this problem, make a plant list by season of bloom. Don't over-complicate things by going month by month—early, mid, and late

Bloom times of some favorite perennials

Early season	Mid season	Late season
Basket of gold (*Aurinia*)	Astilbe	Aster
Bleeding heart (*Dicentra*)	Baby's breath (*Gypsophila*)	Chrysanthemum
Candytuft (*Iberis*)	Bee balm (*Monarda*)	Culver's root (*Veronicastrum*)
Columbine (*Aquilegia*)	Blanket flower (*Gaillardia*)	Globe thistle (*Echinops*)
Cranesbill (*Geranium*)	Coralbell (*Heuchera*)	Goldenrod (*Solidago*)
Creeping phlox (*Phlox subulata*)	Coreopsis (larger and threadleaf types)	Helen's flower (*Helenium*)
Delphinium		Heliopsis
Dianthus	Daylily (*Hemerocallis*)	Joe Pye Weed (*Eupatorium*)
Iris (*Siberian and bearded*)	Drumstick allium (*Allium sphaero-cephalum*)	Japanese anemone (*Anemone x hybrida* and *A. hupehensis*)
Leopard's bane (*Doronicum*)	Gas plant (*Dictamnus*)	Monkshood (*Aconitum*)
Oriental poppy (*Papaver*)	Goat's beard (*Aruncus*)	Ornamental grasses
Ornamental onions (*Alliums*)	Golden marguerite (*Anthemis*)	Prairie coneflower (*Ratibida*)
Peony (*Paeonia*)	Heliopsis	Purple coneflower (*Echinacea*)
Pulmonaria	Liatris	Rubeckia
Primrose (*Primula*)	Lilies (*Lilium*)	Sedum 'Autumn Joy' and 'Matrona'
Rock cress (*Arabis* and *Aubrieta*)	Meadow rue (*Thalictrum*)	Summer phlox (*Phlox paniculata*)
Spring-flowering bulbs	Shasta daisy (*Leucanthemum*)	
Spurge (*Euphorbia*)	Yarrow (*Achillea*)	
Woodland phlox (*Phlox divaricata* and *P. stolonifera*)		

categories for bloom seasons will do—and then pick perennials so you have something flowering through all periods of the growing season. (See box on bloom times on page 83.) A good book on perennials will introduce you to many plants you may not know yet—see the back of this book for some suggestions.

Another technique is to pick plants that bloom at the same time—for example, early-summer-flowering Siberian irises and peonies—and plant them in a group of, say, one peony to three irises. Next to this group, add plants that bloom later—for example, three purple cone-flowers (*Echinacea*) in front of a couple of summer phloxes (*Phlox paniculata*). Between the perennials, plant groups of bulbs such as tulips, daffodils, or alliums (ornamental onions) for early color. Add clumps of long-blooming annuals such as blue salvia or cosmos, and you'll be on your way to color that lasts most of the season.

To keep the garden looking good when plants have finished flowering, choose perennials that have attractive leaves—green is a color too, and leaves also come in other lovely shades, such as burgundy, silver, and lime green. Some perennials in the "neat leaves" category are yarrow, astilbe, peony, Siberian iris, pinks, and ornamental grasses.

Ready, Set, Plant

Once you've prepared the soil in your flower beds (see page 27) and assembled your plants, try a layout before planting. Set each container where you plan to plant it. This helps to space them properly (see the height and spread information on plant tags that come with each container). Then stand back to see if your groupings are working and you have enough plants.

Planting how-to

- The best time to plant annuals and perennials isn't a hot, sunny day but a cooler, cloudier one—such conditions are less stressful for the plants, and the gardener.
- Never shoehorn a plant into a hole that's too small. Dig a hole just wider but no deeper than the container. Soak the hole with water and let it drain away.
- Tap the sides of the container or squeeze it to loosen the root ball. Then hold one hand over top of the soil and turn the container

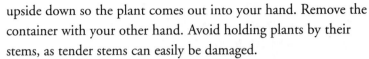

upside down so the plant comes out into your hand. Remove the
container with your other hand. Avoid holding plants by their
stems, as tender stems can easily be damaged.

- Set the plant into the hole, green side up. If roots are circling,
loosen them with your fingers (if the plant is badly root-bound,
use a knife to make several cuts at the sides and one at the base).
The top of the root ball should be at or just below the soil's
surface.
- Cover roots with loose soil, add a little water, then add the remaining soil and pack gently but firmly. Don't put granular fertilizer
into the planting hole, as it can be too caustic for delicate roots.
Instead, give a water-soluble transplanting fertilizer.
- Water well.

Ta da, you've done it! How many left to go?

Plant in fall for spring color: Spring bulbs

Spring-flowering bulbs—tulips, daffodils, hyacinths, crocuses, and
many others, including the gorgeous alliums (ornamental onions)—
are about the easiest plants for beginners. The most important thing
to know? Plant in the fall. They need a winter's nap to perform their
spring magic. The ideal time to plant is when night temperatures fall
to between 40°F to 50°F (5°C to 10°C). But don't leave bulb planting
too late—bulbs need about six weeks before the ground freezes to
make root growth. And, trust me, you don't want to be doing this in
sleet and snow.

BULB BASICS

- Plant in a well-drained bed where bulbs will get full or afternoon
sun in spring. Loosen the soil with a garden fork and remove any
weeds. Dig either a small trench or a wide hole for clusters of
bulbs, or individual holes for individual bulbs. Try to group bulbs
together—isolated loners aren't very effective.
- The bigger the bulb, the deeper it goes. Plant about three to four
times as deep as the height of the bulb—large bulbs about 8" to
10" (20 to 25 cm) and smaller ones about 5" (12.5 cm) deep.
Space bigger bulbs 3" to 10" (7.5 to 25 cm) and small ones 2"
(5 cm) apart.

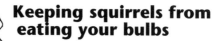

> ### Keeping squirrels from eating your bulbs
>
> If you have problems with thieving squirrels, plant a little deeper than normal, partially cover the bulbs with soil, then put chicken wire over the area and fill with the rest of the soil; bulb stems will grow through the chicken wire. Or stick to daffodils—they taste awful, it's said, and are poisonous to eat, so furry fiends leave them alone.

- Plant pointed side up. Most bulbs are obvious, but some can be tricky. If you're not sure which end is up, don't fret—plant them sideways. They will sort themselves out.
- To finish up, water thoroughly.
- Just before the ground freezes, apply 2" to 3" (5 to 7.5 cm) of mulch (compost, wood chips, or chopped-up leaves). In spring, the bulbs will come up through the mulch.
- Bulbs are fully charged for peak flowering in their first spring, so any fertilizer you give them will benefit them in subsequent seasons. After they've flowered in spring, sprinkle a small amount of slow-release "bulb food" around the plants to supply nutrients for blooming the following year. (Contrary to popular advice, don't put fertilizer in the hole with the bulb when you're planting, as this may burn the bulb's tender roots.) Bonemeal used to be touted as a good bulb fertilizer, but modern bonemeal has few nutrients and, worse, often attracts animals that dig up the bed looking for bones.
- After the flowers have bloomed, snip them off so the plants won't put energy into producing seed. Let the leaves die back naturally for at least six weeks, and don't give in to the temptation to "tidy up" by tying leaves with rubber bands. The leaves are busy recharging the bulb for next year's bloom—they can't soak up the sun if they're gagged and bound. To camouflage dying bulbs, plant them between large perennials that will grow to hide bulb foliage.

The Well-Groomed Flower Garden

Deadheading has nothing to do with a certain rock group—it's hort-speak for a useful technique: removing flowers that have finished blooming. Some plants, especially daylilies and bearded irises, leave

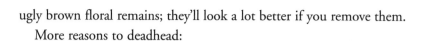

ugly brown floral remains; they'll look a lot better if you remove them. More reasons to deadhead:

- Once flowers are pollinated, they form seeds, which costs the plant energy. By removing faded flowers before seeds form, you encourage energy to go toward new flower, foliage, and root growth instead.
- Some perennials, such as anise hyssop and goldenrod, can soon act like weeds in a garden. By removing potential seeds, you keep them from self-sowing where they're not wanted.
- Deadheading can encourage a second flush of bloom later in the season in some perennials, such as perennial salvias, roses, and delphiniums.
- A related technique is shearing to keep plants neat. For example, by midsummer, many early-blooming plants such as rock cress, perennial candytuft, creeping phlox, catmint and cranesbills (hardy geraniums) grow floppy or leggy. Shearing them back—removing spent flowers and cutting foliage back by half—promotes lush new leaf growth.
- Some plants, such as ornamental grasses and coneflowers (*Rudbeckia* and *Echinacea* species), have attractive seed heads that you can leave in place for winter interest and to attract seed-loving birds. Cut these plants back in early spring before growth starts again.

 Sometimes gardeners have to be cruel—do a little pinching—to be kind. Pinching back perennial asters and mums will make them bushier and less likely to flop, and you'll get more flowers. Pinch back a third to a half of the plant, which simply means using your pruners to cut the plant back. Shape the plant into a pleasing mounded form as you go. Don't pinch after the beginning of July or the plant may not produce buds in time for fall flowering.

Divide and Conquer

If the thought of digging up a favorite perennial and cutting its root ball into pieces makes you weak in the knees, you're not alone. So why do it? There are several reasons:

- **To rejuvenate plants:** After growing for several years, many perennials die back or get old and woody in the middle, while some seem to lose vigor and have fewer flowers. Sometimes you'll see a donut—dieback in the middle and active growth around the outside. By dividing, you're giving the plant a facelift.
- **To control the size of clumps:** When perennial space invaders get too big or grow into neighboring plants, it's time to remedy the situation.

- **To divide and multiply:** Want plants for free? One perennial can be divided into four or five, giving you more plants and allowing for bigger groupings and more design punch. If you don't need them all, give divisions away or trade with friends and neighbors (or just compost them).

When to divide

You can divide plants in early spring or early fall. The general rule is to divide plants that bloom in mid to late summer in spring and early-season bloomers in fall. Some early-spring bloomers are best divided right after they flower so they'll reestablish strongly enough to flower again the following spring—these include creeping phlox, Jacob's ladder, pulmonaria, primrose, and rock cress.

I prefer to divide most plants in spring. You gain an entire season of growth and have stronger plants before winter comes. When you have well-rooted plants, there's less chance of "frost heave"—the action of frost can literally heave newly planted perennials out of the ground over the winter. However, some plants survive early fall division better—these include peonies, bleeding hearts, Oriental poppies, and bearded iris.

Here are some more pointers:

- Make spring divisions when top growth is 2" to 3" (5 to 7.5 cm) tall.
- Divide ornamental grasses in spring while they're still dormant (many won't survive fall division).
- Do fall division in time to allow for six to eight weeks of root growth before a hard frost. Before digging plants up, cut their foliage back to within 2" to 3" (5 to 7.5 cm) of the ground. Add a layer of mulch around plants just before freeze-up to help keep soil temperatures even and minimize frost heave. For fastest re-establishment, make big divisions with good roots.

Doing the deed

You will need:

- a piece of tarp to protect the lawn or patio and simplify cleanup
- a digging spade, shovel or fork
- a rake to level beds when replanting

Division timetable

Perennials to divide every two to three years	Perennials that don't need or don't like division
Aster	Balloon flower (*Platycodon*)
Bearded iris	Bleeding heart (*Dicentra*)
Coreopsis	Columbine (*Aquilegia*)
Cranesbill (*Heuchera sanguinea*)	Gas plant (*Dictamnus*)
Creeping phlox (*Phlox subulata*)	Goat's beard (*Aruncus*)
Golden marguerite (*Anthemis*)	Japanese anemone (*Anenome hupehensis* and *Anenome hybrida*)
Helen's flower (*Helenium autumnale*)	Lupin (*Lupinus*)
Pinks (*Dianthus*)	Mallow (*Malva*)
Rock cress (*Arabis caucasica*)	Peony (*Paeonia*)
Shasta daisy (*Leucanthemum* x *superbum*)	Poppy (*Papaver*)
Snow-in-summer (*Cerastium*)	Russian sage (*Perovskia*)
Summer phlox (*Phlox paniculata*)	Sea holly (*Eryngium*)
Yarrow (*Achillea*)	

- a knife or a handsaw for tough clumps (daylilies, hosta)
- an axe for the really tough customers, such as large ornamental grasses (really!)
- a hose and a source of water

Now here's how to proceed:

1. If the weather has been very dry, water plants to be divided the day before.
2. Cut into the soil with your spade about 4" to 8" (10 to 20 cm) from the edge of the plant's crown, then dig around and under the entire plant before lifting it carefully.
3. Place the plant on the tarp and remove any dead, woody material.
4. Take new divisions from vigorously growing outer sections. Some plants fall apart easily. Shasta daisies, asters, bee balm, or lamb's ears can be divided into pieces by hand, while others—astilbe, hosta, and Siberian iris—require a sharp knife.

5. Set divisions in a shady spot and protect the roots from drying out with a damp piece of burlap until replanting. You're better off replanting as soon as possible, but if you can't, pot your divisions up in spare nursery pots and store them in a shady spot, keeping them well watered.

6. To replant, work in soil enrichments like compost or well-rotted manure, rake the bed level, and plant the divisions, leaving enough space for growth (spacing depends on the height and spread of the plant at maturity).

7. Water with a dose of water-soluble transplant fertilizer.

Flower Garden Tune-Up

Don't worry if it takes several seasons to get things looking the way you'd imagined—that's perfectly normal. When the garden doesn't meet your expectations, ask yourself the following questions:

- **Are the planting areas all over the place?** Look at the entire yard, not just the individual planting beds. Try to link beds, rather than having one here and another over there.

- **Are the beds too narrow?** A thin bed isn't wide enough to show off layers of plants. If you have a skinny bed that can't be widened, between a hedge and a walkway, for instance, fill it with low-growing ground cover plants of one or two kinds—not a hodgepodge mix.

- **Have you crammed in too many types of plants?** You'll get more impact from plants if you put three of one type in a clump, rather than three different plants or three of the same plant in different locations. Repetition of key plant groups or a key color creates harmony and coherence.

- **Have you screened eyesores?** Treat the space around your house as a garden, not a yard. Your backdrop should complement your plants. Make storage sheds or garage walls into garden features (vine-covered trellises can hide ugly ones). Be sure to screen utilitarian necessities like the compost pile, air-conditioning units, heat pumps, and so on with attractive fences or evergreen shrubs.

- **Do the garden and house seem divorced from each other?** Look out the windows to make sure the picture is pleasing from inside the house too.

- **Do you have a focal point?** Add contrasts in texture and form—bigger leaves next to fine ones, or spiky flowers next to rounded and mounded ones. You could be asking plants to do all the work; perhaps the missing element is what garden designers call a "focal point." Try adding a bird bath, a sundial, an arbor, or a trellis. And of course no garden is complete without a bench. Or two.

Chapter 9

Made for the Shade: When Your Garden Doesn't Get Much Sun

The grass *is* always greener on the other side of the fence. In my old stamping grounds, I used to envy the shady yard that belonged to the neighbor behind me. On hot, humid days, you could sit comfortably in her garden—which was inconceivable in my sizzling, sun-drenched plot. Human nature being what it is, my neighbor found her shade frustrating and hired somebody to chop away at a large tree, disfiguring it in the process, because she wanted to grow colorful, sun-loving roses and peonies. The plants she lusted after thrived in my sunny garden, of course, while I had a tiny bit of shade cast by the north wall of my house and would have been thrilled to have more. I'm sure my neighbor and I would have gladly traded yards if we could.

The simple fact of the matter is that the sun doesn't shine equally on all gardens and a lot of new gardeners are either frustrated or intimidated by shade—a mindset that almost certainly stems from the typical first encounter with a treed back yard that's got brick-hard soil and the remnants of a lawn struggling in the shadows. If grass won't even grow there, how can anything else? But shade doesn't have to be

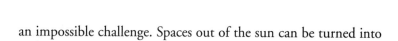

an impossible challenge. Spaces out of the sun can be turned into lush, appealing gardens.

Getting plants to grow well in shade is elementary. Again, it goes back to adding humus to the soil (see Chapter 3), and of course choosing plants that tolerate or prefer low-light conditions.

The Secrets of Shade Garden Soil

The hard-packed, dead-looking soil often found under backyard trees probably got that way because of our general neatnik habit of carting away fallen leaves and all other plant debris. The result? Soil that's starved of humus.

In natural woodlands, where nobody rakes up, nutrients are constantly recycled into rich layers of humus, so the cure for the nutrient-poor patch of soil under your backyard trees is to add organic matter. Spread 3" (7.5 cm) inches of compost, well-rotted manure, or leaf mold (decomposed leaves) over the soil. You can also add peat moss, but because it contains few soil nutrients and is quite dry, be sure to dampen and mix it with one of the other forms of humus.

But enough is enough. Avoid raising the soil under trees too much or piling soil around the base of the trunk. Try to dig the organic matter into the soil, if possible. If you have networks of thick tree roots, you may find it's impossible to dig anything in without killing yourself and doing major damage to tree roots. If that's your situation, just layer the organic material of your choice over the soil and then plant. That's what I did in my new garden, where the only spot for shade-loving plants was under a grove of pine and spruce trees— not ideal, but it is the only shade I had. Adding humus has worked wonders: As long as I water during dry periods, the shade plants— which include hostas, foamflowers, and other woodland plants—thrive.

Shade gardens take their cue from nature

If you walk through a natural woodland, you'll notice the plants are arranged in layers: At the top comes the tree canopy, then an understory of smaller trees and shrubs that enjoy dappled light, and, finally, at ground level, perennials and flowering plants. Shrubs fill out shade beds and provide interest in winter when perennials are dormant. Be sure to plant them where they get light dappled shade.

REALITY CHECK

Myth: People often complain that nothing will grow under large pine or spruce trees because dropped needles turn the soil acidic over time.

Fact: The real reason many plants don't thrive under large evergreens is dense shade and extreme dryness.

The cure: If you plant perennials where they face dry shade conditions, water deeply and frequently, and layer mulch over the soil. If all else fails, put shade-loving plants in containers and use those under your evergreen tree instead. (For more on dry shade, see page 97.)

Shade-tolerant shrubs

Deciduous	Evergreens and broadleaf evergreens
Fothergilla (*Fothergilla gardenii*)	Boxwood (*Buxus*)
Japanese kerria (*Kerria japonica*)	Euonymus
Oak-leaf hydrangea (*Hydrangea quercifolia*)	Holly (*Ilex*)
	Azalea and Rhododendron*
Serviceberry (*Amelanchier*)	Yew (*Taxus*)
Silver-leaved dogwood (*Cornus alba* 'Elegantissima')	
Sweet pepper bush (*Clethra alnifolia*)	*need acidic soil

Planting Your Shady Garden

To begin, let the outlines of your bed follow shadow lines cast by the trees or buildings. For planting under trees, I use a spade with a narrow blade or my trusty trowel substitute, the Ho-Mi digger. To tuck the plants in between tree roots, I find small plants sold in 4" (10 cm) pots are easier than larger ones—the smaller the planting holes, the less you have to chop away at tree roots—and it's a good idea to work

in a little extra humus as you dig holes for individual plants. Give them some transplant fertilizer and water them well.

To finish the job, imitate nature by sprinkling leaves around the bed as mulch. If you shred them first (either with a leaf shredder or by running the mower over them), they won't mat and will decompose faster. I use leaves I collect from a huge weeping willow nearby that are so small they don't need to be shredded. A couple of inches of wood chips or shredded bark mulch on top of the bed will make good mulch if you don't have leaves. Mulch helps keep the soil moist and turns into humus as it decomposes (which also means you'll have to add a new layer every couple of years). Just be sure to keep the stuff off the crowns of the perennials and keep it a few inches away from tree trunks.

One more task will get your plants off to a good start and keep them going: water regularly, especially during dry periods. Trees guzzle moisture and leave precious little for other plants growing under them. But here's something you're going to like: Aside from watering and mulching, shade gardens are a cinch to take care of because the lower light levels and the layer of mulch put a damper on weed germination. So what's not to like about shade?

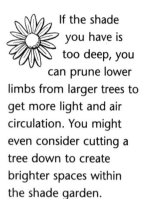 If the shade you have is too deep, you can prune lower limbs from larger trees to get more light and air circulation. You might even consider cutting a tree down to create brighter spaces within the shade garden.

Light by Degrees

Plant tags say things like "sun or part shade" or "full shade." So what exactly do they mean?

Light shade

Where sunlight is filtered through the canopy of small-leaved trees, you get dappled shade. Trees with high canopies also give light shade. Some plants listed for sun will do fine with this amount of light, especially in hotter regions where their foliage can get scorched in full sun. Here are a few you could try:

 **Light-shade plants**

Annuals and biennials	Perennials
Browallia	Astilbe or false spirea (*Astible* x *arendsii*)
Flowering tobacco (*Nicotiana* species)	Bear's breeches (*Acanthus mollis*)
Foxglove (*Digitalis purpurea*)	Coral bells (*Heuchera*)
Impatiens	Ivy-leaf cyclamen (*Cyclamen hederifolium*)
Johnny-jump-up (*Viola tricolor*)	Lady's mantle (*Alchemilla mollis*)
Larkspur	Siberian iris (*Iris siberica*)
Tuberous and wax begonias	Virginia bluebell (*Mertensia virginica*)
	Yellow corydalis (*Corydalis lutea*)

Part or semi-shade

Plants preferring this level of light typically need protection from sun at midday, when the light is strongest. Either put them where they get sun in the morning but shade in the afternoon or plant them where they'll get filtered light but not direct sun. A few suggestions include:

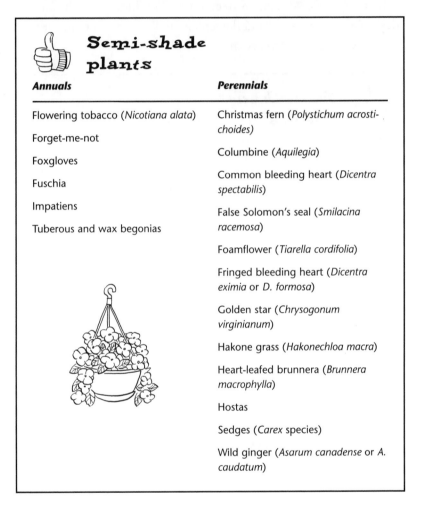

Semi-shade plants

Annuals	Perennials
Flowering tobacco (*Nicotiana alata*)	Christmas fern (*Polystichum acrosti-choides*)
Forget-me-not	
Foxgloves	Columbine (*Aquilegia*)
Fuschia	Common bleeding heart (*Dicentra spectabilis*)
Impatiens	False Solomon's seal (*Smilacina racemosa*)
Tuberous and wax begonias	
	Foamflower (*Tiarella cordifolia*)
	Fringed bleeding heart (*Dicentra eximia* or *D. formosa*)
	Golden star (*Chrysogonum virginianum*)
	Hakone grass (*Hakonechloa macra*)
	Heart-leafed brunnera (*Brunnera macrophylla*)
	Hostas
	Sedges (*Carex* species)
	Wild ginger (*Asarum canadense* or *A. caudatum*)

Full or deep shade

Full shade is often found under large evergreens, under deciduous trees with low branches or a dense crown, or close to the north wall of a building—all these provide places for confirmed shade lovers. Sometimes deep shade combines with partial shade or even full sun in early spring before deciduous trees leaf out, so this can also be an ideal spot to grow woodland flowers and bulbs that bloom in early spring. Among your choices are:

Full-shade plants

Annuals	Perennials
Caladium	Bloodroot (*Sanguinaria canadensis*)
Coleus	Bugleweed (*Ajuga reptans*)
Impatiens	European ginger (*Asarum europaeum*)
	Maidenhair fern (*Adiantum pedatum*)
	Periwinkle (*Vinca minor*)
	Solomon's seal (*Polygonatum* species)
	Spurge, Japanese and Allegheny spurge (*Pachysandra* species)
	Trilliums

Leaves of Shade

When I started gardening, it was all about color and flowers—but the longer I stay at it, the more pleasure I take in foliage. Shade plants tend to have large leaves to capture as much sunlight as possible, so rather than obsessing about flowers, sophisticated shade gardeners tend to emphasize leaf shapes, textures, and colors. The not-so-sophisticated ones just plant umpteen impatiens—not that there's anything wrong with this popular annual (though garden snobs love to hate it). Impatiens is much loved precisely because it likes shade and blooms all season long. Clumps of soft-colored impatiens are lovely among shade perennials—it's just that a steady diet of nothing but impatiens gets a tad predictable, not to mention that they're definitely more work to plant every year than perennials.

Five ways to get the most out of lush leaves

1. Play shapes against each other to create pleasing plant pictures. For example, combine the grassy, strap-like leaves of Siberian iris with plants that have bold, heart-shaped or rounded leaves, such as hostas or bergenias.
2. Contrast simple, bold leaf shapes such as those found in hostas with plants that have lacy compound leaves, such as astilbes or ferns.
3. Plant in groups for the best effect. A generous drift of five astilbes or ferns will have more impact next to a large specimen hosta than just one or two lonely little astilbes or ferns.
4. Use foliage plants, especially those with interesting leaf colors. In addition to hostas, which come in a variety of leaf colors, there are shade-loving ornamental grasses such as golden hakone grass (*Hakonechloa macra* 'Aureola'), golden and bronze sedges (*Carex* species), and pulmonaria, which comes in lovely leaf shades of shimmering silver.
5. Variegated leaves—foliage with distinct markings such as white or yellow on green—add a touch of brightness to a shady area. But avoid stuffing your garden full of too many variegated plants. A noted British gardener who tried this ended up calling his variegated plot "the insane asylum." Plants with white variegation do well in deeper shade, while plants with yellow variegation have a better yellow color if they get light or dappled shade.

Queen of the Shade: Heavenly Hosta

Hosta ho-hum? No way—hostas are hot. Not long ago, if you had a green- or blue-leaved hosta and one with white edges, that was it. Now, thanks largely to North American hosta enthusiasts and plant breeders, you can find hundreds of different cultivars, ranging from the colorfully named chartreuse 'Abba Dabba Do' to the large, metallic gold 'Zounds.' In between, there are scores of green, variegated, gold, and blue-leaved types in sizes from tiny to mammoth.

Native to Japan, Korea, and China, these members of the lily family are deservedly popular—they're easy to grow, tough, cold-hardy, and shade-tolerant. And, unlike some perennials, hostas just get better with age: Clumps grow larger, margins on variegated leaves become wider, puckering or seersucker patterns on leaves become more outstanding, and foliage color intensifies, especially in the blue- and gold-toned cultivars.

Mostly grown for their foliage, hostas flower in shades from white to mauve. In my opinion, the best flowers are found on the cultivar 'Fragrant Bouquet'—its white, trumpet-like flowers appear in late summer and have a heady, gardenia-like fragrance. In size, hostas range from petite, such as 'Pixie Power', under 2" inches (5 cm) tall, to giant—both the gold 'Sum and Substance' and the mammoth blue 'Krossa Regal' grow into clumps 4' to 5' (1.2 to 1.5 m) wide. But be patient: It can take three or more years for a hosta bought in a standard nursery pot to grow to a showy size.

Here are some things to consider:

- Smaller varieties, up to 12" (30 cm) tall, make good edgers along paths or the front of a bed. Medium-sized ones make excellent ground covers, and large hostas are terrific as background or dramatic accent plants.
- Use variegated hostas—cultivars with markings or edgings of white, cream, or gold—to light up shady corners.
- Look for hostas with thick leaves (the plant tag may use the term "good substance") to avoid problems with snails and slugs chewing holes in the foliage.
- Leave enough room for their size at maturity.
- Mature hostas rarely need dividing, but you can divide them to increase your supply. Dig the clump up with a strong spade and use a sharp knife to cut it into divisions for replanting into the garden.

How shady are these characters?

Hostas make great low-maintenance perennials for shade, but most of them grow better and bigger with some sun, as long as they get

plentiful moisture. Morning sun with filtered shade in the afternoon is ideal. A few pointers:

- Gold- and green-leaved types and many variegated varieties need some sun to develop good foliage color.
- Blue-leaved varieties grow best in moist, shady conditions. Avoid planting them where afternoon sun is intense.
- Too much sun and not enough moisture can cause foliage to bleach out or scorch.

Control the hosta enemy: slugs

Hostas are generally care-free plants, with one big exception: slugs and snails, those slimy nocturnal critters that eat holes in leaves. The moister the climate, the worse the problem. To outwit slugs:

- Choose resistant varieties. Look for plant tag descriptions such as "slug resistant" or "good substance," meaning the cultivar has thick dense leaves with a waxy coating. Fortunately, slug-resistant hostas tend to be the most desirable and attractive ones.
- Put stale beer into a saucer set in the ground near plants to attract and drown slugs.
- Check out commercial slug baits. The older types containing metaldehyde have to be used with extreme caution, as they can poison birds, pets, and even small children. The newer slug baits containing iron phosphate are a lot safer.
- An alternative is to fill a spray bottle with one part ammonia to nine parts water, a solution that kills slugs but avoids the risk of toxic residue. Spray in early spring just before hostas leaf out.

Coping with Dry Shade

Trees have root systems that spread beyond the crown, and such roots are strong competitors for soil nutrients and moisture. You're most likely to find dry shade under trees with wide-spreading, shallow roots, such as Norway maple, beech, and willow, and, of course, evergreen trees. To give your shade plants the best possible chance under such conditions, water deeply and fertilize more often than you normally would.

Most shade plants prefer moist soil, so dry shade is a special

👍 Spring-flowering bulbs for the shade

Many bulbs disappear in the summer—a clever adaptation to drier, shadier conditions—but thrive in the sunny conditions under deciduous trees in early spring before the leaves come out. Besides tulips and daffodils, try:

- windflower (*Anemone blanda*)
- glory-of-the-snow (*Chionodoxa*)
- crocus
- snowdrops (*Galanthus*)
- winter aconite (*Eranthus*)
- grape hyacinth (*Muscari*)
- Siberian squills (*Scilla*)

---

challenge for gardeners. The following plants will perk up a dry, shady spot in your garden—which is not to say that they prefer dryness, just that they'll do better than other shade plants. But be sure to water well while they're getting established.

Survivor perennials for dry shade

If these plants don't work, or you want to do the least amount of work possible, you can just take the path of least resistance and put a layer of mulch under your trees. But you do want to give this kind of garden a try—right?

- **Barren strawberry (*Waldsteinia*):** A low-growing, dense mat of leaves that slightly resemble those of strawberries.
- **Big-root geranium (*Geranium macrorrhizum*):** Attractive and aromatic leaves, flowers in late spring in colors ranging from white to pink and magenta, depending on cultivar. Not to be confused with the common annual geraniums of the genus *Pelargonium*.
- **Bishop's hat, or barrenwort (*Epimedium* x *versicolor*):** Attractive heart-shaped leaves. With its delicate yellow flowers, 'Sulphureum' is the most popular cultivar.
- **Dead nettle (*Lamium maculatum*):** Look for cultivars such as 'Beacon Silver' with rosy pink flowers and silver leaves edged in green or the white-blooming 'White Nancy.'

- **Heart-leaved bergenia (*Bergenia cordifolia*):** Large, leathery leaves and rose-pink flowers in early spring; looks great in a big grouping.
- **Sweet woodruff (*Galium odoratum*):** Finely textured leaves and white flowers in spring; top-flight ground cover in dry shade.
- **Ground cover plants:** To make it really easy, consider the big three ground covers—ivy, pachysandra, and periwinkle—which are all tough evergreen perennial plants. (See pages 69–70.)

Chapter 10

The Big Picture: Trees, Shrubs, and Vines

It seems odd that people will spend weeks researching floor coverings or paint colors but take just 10 minutes to pick out a tree that could easily gobble up most of their garden real estate. Planting a tree is a lot like getting married—you hope the relationship will last a lifetime, so it's doubly important to choose wisely. Keep in mind that a tree is about the only plant that can outlive you and your spouse.

First, think about what you want in a tree—a leafy canopy for shade, a spring-flowering focal point, or an elegant evergreen that looks good year-round? Maybe you have room for them all (though chances are that you don't).

If you have a bare yard, read on for suggestions on choosing and planting trees and shrubs. On the other hand, if you've inherited a bunch of trees and shrubs, and you have no idea what most of them are—and you already hate at least half of them—there's a game plan for you at the end of the chapter. But do read about pruning first, though, so you'll know what you're doing and why.

Trees and shrubs lend grace to the landscape. In the city, they soften asphalt and concrete surroundings; in any garden, they give shade and privacy screening, dampen noise, and offer home and shelter for birds (and pesky squirrels, but who's perfect?). All trees have environmental benefits, but large, hard-wooded deciduous varieties offer maximum benefits: They clean and oxygenate air (think of them as the earth's lungs) and provide coolness through shade and evaporation but allow warming sun through in winter. Windbreak evergreens can reduce heating bills by deflecting cold winds.

There. If that doesn't make you want to run out and get planting, what would?

Did You Know?

Trees can increase the value of your house by up to 20%. Planting attractive trees in a bare yard is guaranteed to pay back in curb appeal—and that's a good thing, considering how often many of us move.

So Many Trees, So Little Space!

Before you shop, consider soil and moisture conditions, hardiness zone, whether there's sun or shade, and, most important, how much room there is above and below ground for natural growth. Beautiful trees can become liabilities if they're planted in the wrong place. You've seen the results—blue spruce syndrome—behemoth evergreens looming menacingly over captive houses, shutting out all traces of sunlight. Hard to believe they started out as cute Christmas trees, isn't

Help!

What's the difference between a tree and a shrub?

To the uninitiated, they're bushes, but let's call a shrub a shrub.

Shrubs have several stems, and many species (the ones everybody's always hacking back) can easily grow as wide and tall as a small tree. Trees have a single stem (trunk) and grow reasonably tall. Most trees grow from the tips of their branches. Shrubs do that too, but most also send out new stems from the ground. But sometimes the difference may not be so clear: You'll find multi-stemmed trees and shrubs that have been trained to a single stem.

it? Woody plants are on a mission—to grow bigger. They won't stay the size they were at the nursery—guaranteed!

Tree planting dos and don'ts

- Plant at least 20' (6 m) away from the house or garage.
- Unless you have a country estate, resist trees that get humungous: weeping willows, horse chestnuts, London plane trees, and most large maples and oaks will all overwhelm a small garden faster than you can imagine.
- Avoid planting large trees where they'll grow into power lines, underground utilities, or your house foundation.
- Don't put a tree that drops flowers or berries near patios, driveways, or sidewalks.
- Fast-growing trees—poplars and silver maples, for example—are tempting when you've got a bare yard, but they tend to be weak-wooded and short-lived. If you plant fast growers, balance them with better trees and be prepared to cut the speedy trees down before they become liabilities.

Choosing Compatible Trees and Shrubs

Climate and growing conditions vary widely across North America, so putting together a suitable list of plants would take another book. Below, you'll find some recommendations for attractive trees and first-rate shrubs. The list includes more trees in the smaller categories because most properties don't have space for huge trees. To give you more adventurous planting choices, my recommendations include top-rate plants that should be better known—you'll be one up on the neighbors right from the start.

Decisions, decisions, decisions

EVERGREEN OR DECIDUOUS?

Try to have evergreens make up about a third of your garden to give it life over the winter, but don't overdo large evergreen trees—too many can turn your garden gloomy. Evergreens come in two cate-

gories—needled (the familiar pines and spruces) and broadleaf (box-wood, rhododendron, and holly)—though, nature being nature, there are exceptions: Larches and dawn redwoods look like evergreens, but they lose their leaves. Most evergreen shrubs are cold-hardy, but few broadleaf evergreens tolerate the bitter winters of zone 4 and colder.

OTHER ORNAMENTAL QUALITIES

Consider attractive flowers, leaf shapes and colors, fall color or berries, and, most important, hardiness and disease resistance. For example, the popular white-barked paper birches (*Betula papyrifera*)

👍 Shade trees

Heritage river birch (*Betula nigra* 'Heritage')	A good native birch that's pest- and disease-resistant. Attractive, peeling bark. Needs a spot that is moist in spring. Zones 4 to 9.
Katsura (*Cercidiphyllum japonicum*)	Medium sized. Elegant, heart-shaped leaves give good yellow fall color. A good tree for urban yards. Zones 4 to 8.
Sweet gum (*Liquidamber styraciflua*)	Attractive, deep green, glossy maple-like leaves that turn scarlet, yellow, or orange in fall. Interesting corky bark. Zones 5 to 9.
Yellowwood (*Cladrastis kentuckea*)	Handsome, bright green leaves that turn yellow in fall. White flowers in late spring. Zones 4 to 8.

👍 Small flowering or accent trees

Carolina silverbell (*Halesia Carolina*)	White, bell-shaped flowers in spring. Will tolerate some shade. Hardy from zones 4 to 8.
Crabapple (*Malus* hybrids)	Copious flowers and fruits, both highly ornamental. Look for disease-resistant varieties: 'Adams,' 'Indian Summer,' 'Donald Wyman,' 'Prairie Fire,' 'Sugar Tyme,' 'White Angel,' *zumi* var. *calocarpa*. Zones 3 to 8, depending on cultivar.
Eastern redbud (*Cercis canadensis*)	Beautiful early-spring-flowering tree native to eastern North America. Small, rosy purple flowers before leaves emerge. Grows well in part shade. Zones 5 to 9.
Fringe tree (*Chionanthus virginicus*)	A profusion of white flowers in late spring, golden-yellow fall color. Zones 3 to 9.
Ivory silk tree (*Syringa reticulata* 'Ivory Silk')	Produces creamy, honey-scented flowers after other lilacs have bloomed. Shiny, cherry-like bark attractive in winter. Zones 3 to 7.
Japanese maple (*Acer plamatum*)	Many attractive varieties, some with dark reddish leaves such as 'Bloodgood.' 'Dissectum' varieties are more shrub-like with fine lacy foliage. Zones 5 to 8.

Small flowering or accent trees (continued)

Magnolia	Great small trees for spring flowers, including star magnolia, *Magnolia stellata* 'Royal Star' (white flowers), and Loebner magnolia 'Leonard Messel' (white flowers with pink markings). "The Girls" hybrids, all given girl's names ('Ann,' 'Betty,' 'Jane,' 'Judy,' 'Pinkie,' 'Randy,' 'Ricki,' and 'Susan'), flower in the pink to purple range. Zones 4 to 8.
Serviceberry, or shadblow (*Amelanchier* hybrids)	White flowers in early spring, blue-black edible berries, orange to red fall color. Tolerates light shade and grows well on the east side of taller trees. Zones 3 to 7, depending on cultivar.

Evergreen trees

Black Hills spruce *Picea glauca* var. *densata*	Clean Christmas-tree-like form. Narrow, dense, slow growth, keeps in scale where other spruces become overgrown. Tolerant of hot, dry summers and cold winters. Zones 2 to 6.
Concolor fir (*Abies concolor*)	Slow-growing, with beautiful long, curved bluish-green needles. Creates softer effect than blue spruce but grows large, so be careful where you plant it. Zones 3 to 7.
Serbian spruce (*Picea omerika*)	One of the most graceful spruces, with an attractive narrow form and drooping branches. Zones 4 to 7.
Weeping nootka false cypress (*Chamaecyparis nootkatensis* 'Pendula')	Excellent specimen tree. Upright habit and graceful hanging branches make it dramatic and unusual. Dark green. Attractive all year. Zones 4 to 7.

tend to be short-lived in many regions because their wood is lunch and dinner to an insect called the bronze birch borer, but the Heritage river birch (*Betula nigra* 'Heritage') is resistant.

To learn more about woody plants

There are hundreds of attractive trees, shrubs, and vines available to gardeners today. Keep in mind that diversity is also good for the environment, so don't just plant what the neighbors have. If you're lucky enough to live near a botanical or public garden, look around. They usually label their plants—a huge help. There are also excellent books to consult (for suggestions, see page 187).

Deciduous flowering shrubs by size

Compact—to 3' (1 m)	Medium—to 6' (1.8 m)	Large—over 6' (1.8 m)
Annabelle Hydrangea (*Hydrangea arborescens* 'Annabelle'): white pom-pom like flowers in mid-summer. Zones 2 to 8.	Meyer lilac (*Syringa meyeri* 'Palibin'): fragrant blue-purple flowers in early summer. Mildew-resistant. Zones 3 to 7.	Doublefile viburnum 'Mariesii' (*Viburnum plicatum var. tomentosum* 'Mariesii'): large white flowers in late spring. Attractive horizontal branching. Zones 5 to 8.
Dwarf deutzia (*Deutzia gracilis* 'Nikko'): white flowers in spring. Zones 5 to 8.	Pearl bush (*Exochorda macrantha* 'The Bride'): beautiful strings of white, pearl-like flowers in early spring. Zones 5 to 8.	Lilac (*Syringa*): fragrant spring-flowering shrubs in pink, white, lavender, or bluish shades. Choose from early hyacinthifloras, mid spring French hybrids, and late Preston hybrids. Zones 2 to 7.
Japanese spirea (*Spirea japonica*): 'Goldflame,' 'Little Princess,' and 'Shirobana' flower in a variety of pinkish shades in summer and have good fall color. Zones 2 to 8.	Summer snowflake viburnum (*Viburnum plicatum* 'Summer Snowflake'): white lace-cap flowers throughout summer. Zones 5 to 8.	Oak-leaf hydragea (*Hydrangea quercifolia*): upright clusters of white flowers in late summer, oak-like leaves with good fall color. Zones 5 to 9.
Potentilla (*Potentilla fruticosa*): yellow, white, and pink flowering forms available that bloom from early summer to frost. Zones 2 to 7.	Summersweet, or sweet pepper, bush (*Clethra alnifolia*): fragrant white flowers in midsummer. Zones 3 to 9.	Weigela (*Weigela florida*): Pink, reddish pink, or white trumpet-shaped flowers in spring. Zones 4 to 8.

When to Plant Trees and Shrubs

The best time was 20 years ago, and the second best time is right now.

Seriously, as long as you buy from a quality seller who looks after plants properly and the plants are in containers, you can plant anytime during the growing season. Early spring and early to mid fall are the preferred times, however, because temperatures are cooler and rainfall more plentiful—conditions ideal for new root growth. Some trees do better when planted in spring: magnolia, katsura, dogwood, beech, tulip tree (*Lirodendron tulipifera*), yellowwood, and most maples and oaks. Summer planting is trickier because of the heat and dryness but can be successful if you pay close attention to watering. If you're going on holidays, get someone to look after this job.

Evergreen and broadleaf evergreen shrubs

Evergreen

Cedar, or arborvitae (*Thuja*): many rounded and upright forms available. Good hedging plants. Zones 2 to 8.

Dwarf hemlock (*Tsuga canadensis*): soft green foliage. Slow-growing weeping forms include 'Cole' and 'Jeddeloh.' Zones 3 to 7.

False cypress (*Chamaecyparis*): many shrub cultivars available in dwarf forms. Golden, blue, or green foliage. Zones 4 to 8.

Juniper (*Juniperus*): numerous species and their cultivars available, from low and spreading to strongly upright. Zones 3 to 7.

Yew (*Taxus*): dark green foliage. Versatile. Makes good hedge plant. Zones 4 to 7.

Broadleaf evergreen

Blue holly (*Ilex* x *meserveae* cultivars): For good berries on female plants, you need a male plant nearby. Zones 5 to 7.

Lily-of-the-valley shrub (*Pieris japonica*): hanging white or rose-pink flower clusters in spring. Needs acidic soil. Zones 5 to 8.

Oregon grape holly (*Mahonia aquifolium*): bright yellow flowers in spring, holly-like leaves turn bronzy in cold-winter regions. Zones 5 to 8.

Rhododendron (*Rhododendron* species): spring-flowering. Many species and cultivars available, *Rhododendron catawbiense* and 'PJM' types among the hardiest. Needs acidic soil. Zones 4 to 7.

Winter creeper (*Euonymus fortunei*): many cultivars in green or with white or yellow variegated leaves. Zones 4 to 8 (needs snow cover or winter protection in zone 4).

Shopping Checklist

For all woody plants, look for healthy bark free of wounds and healthy, well-colored leaves or intact plump buds if the plant hasn't leafed out yet. Steer clear of plants that look like they've been homeless at the nursery for too long. Check trees that are going to grow into large shade trees for a single central leader, the dominant shoot that carries growth upward. (However, multi-stemmed smaller ornamental trees, such as Japanese maples, won't have a central leader.)

Here are a few things to look for:

- With container-grown plants, check that the roots don't circle too much—circling roots can girdle and kill other roots and put pressure on the bark at the lower trunk.
- Field-grown trees come balled and burlapped (B&B). This means the roots and the surrounding soil are held in place by burlap and sometimes a wire basket. The diameter of the root ball should be 10 to 12 times the diameter of the trunk, and root balls should be flat on top and feel firm.

- When buying any tree, a flare—a slight widening—should be obvious at the base of trunk. If you can't see it, the tree may be planted too deeply in the container, which can lead to rotting of the bark that should not have been covered.
- If the trunk is wrapped, look underneath for injuries, such as wounds, or insect damage. (Wrapping is used to protect the trunk for transportation, but be sure to remove it after planting—bark needs to breathe.)
- With trees, your best buy is a small to medium-sized tree. Large trees are hard to move and expensive to plant (been there, done that—the root balls weigh a ton, and you need heavy equipment, muscles, and nerves of steel). On top of everything else, while a big tree is overcoming transplant shock and regrowing its roots (around 80% of the roots are chopped off when they're dug), the smaller tree is merrily catching up.

Ready, Set, Plant

Before you grab your shovel, be sure you know where all the underground utilities are located. It's annoying to chop through a telephone cable, but hitting an underground gas or power line is something you don't want to do—ever. If there's any question of underground lines, call before you dig.

To avoid damage when moving the tree, always lift it by the root ball or container, never by the trunk. And, as the old saying goes, you're better off putting a $50 tree in a $100 hole than a $100 tree in a $50 hole. To plant, follow these steps:

1. Find the trunk flare—it should be visible after planting. Measure from the truck flare to the bottom of the pot or root ball to get an idea of how deep to dig. Dig a *broad, shallow* planting hole three times as wide as diameter of the root ball but no deeper than the root ball or the container—the hole should resemble a saucer, not a pail. You're better off to plant 2" (5 cm) high to allow for settling.
2. Carefully remove the plant from its container, if it's a plastic one. With a fiber container, to be on the safe side, it's better to put the tree, container and all, in the hole, and then cut the container away with a utility knife.

Many trees and shrubs are grown in the warmer parts of the U.S. because their longer growing seasons make it cheaper and quicker to produce plants there. While southern-grown trees and shrubs may be hardy enough in more northerly regions once they're established, at planting time they are often way ahead in leafing out and flowering and not "hardened off" enough for the cool spring weather. If you buy trees or shrubs that have leafed out early at the nursery, keep them sheltered and plant after the last frost date to prevent injury from late-spring frosts.

3. If the plant is balled and burlapped (B&B), don't loosen or remove anything until you've positioned it in the hole. Check from all directions and straighten the plant before removing the string and burlap and uncovering the top third of root ball. Cut away at least one third of the wire with wire cutters or bolt cutters and as much burlap as you can, but leave the remaining burlap in place to avoid having the root ball fall apart; this material should break down naturally.

4. Fill the hole about one third full and pack soil down gently but firmly—no stomping on the roots, please! You don't have to add extra peat moss or compost, just use your garden soil. Finish backfilling, adding a bit of soil at a time, packing it down and then watering to help it settle. Continue until the hole is filled.

5. Spread a circle of mulch around the base of the tree to at least 3½' to 4' (1 to 1.2 m) out from the trunk. Good choices are leaf litter, pine needles, shredded bark, or wood chips. (Stone mulches or commercial landscape fabrics keep weeds down, but they don't benefit the soil.) Don't mulch too thickly—a 3" to 4" (7.5 to 10 cm) layer is ideal, but more can starve roots of oxygen. Keep the area right against the base of the trunk clear of mulch. When it's up against bark, mulch creates moisture buildup that can lead to decay.

New trees have been treated as invalids for so long you may be surprised to learn that, in most cases, staking is not necessarily a good thing. Studies have shown that trees establish more quickly and develop stronger trunk and root systems if they are *not* staked.

The message? Stake only if your site is very windy or if you're concerned about vandalism. Use two stakes and a wide, flexible tie to reduce chances of injury to the bark, and then leave the stakes in place for *one growing season only*. Spread the word in your neighborhood—especially if you see trees that have been staked and forgotten.

Prescription for the Care and Feeding of New Trees and Shrubs

- Water at least once a week if there isn't enough rain—give the equivalent of 1" inch (25 mm) every seven to 10 days. But don't kill with kindness: Some people drown their new plants.
- Don't fertilize until the second growing season.
- Do minor pruning only to remove dead twigs or damaged branches, then no more until after a year of growth in the new location. Take off too much and you set the plant back (the leaves make food, remember?)

REALITY CHECK

Myth: Prune at least one third of the top growth to compensate for root loss when transplanting.

Fact: This advice is out of date and just plain wrong. (See "Pruning 101," below, for tips on pruning young trees.)

Mulch, mulch, mulch your trees and shrubs

Mulch has so much going for it you have to wonder why everybody doesn't use it. Horticultural scientists at Michigan State University studying new tree plantings in Detroit and Lansing found available soil moisture to be 25% to 50% higher with mulch than without. Other benefits include reducing competition from grass and weeds, and ensuring that you keep string trimmers and mowers well away from vulnerable bark.

Pruning 101: A Clip in Time Saves Nine

Funny, isn't it, that the most common question when buying trees or shrubs is, "How do I prune it?" when a more sensible one would be, "How big will it grow?"

If you have to prune a shrub three or four times a season, it is in the wrong place—stop pruning this instant and remove it or transplant to a spot where it can get as high and wide as it's supposed to.

In its place, plant a shrub that's a better fit. Your garden is not an old-age home for has-been woodies. Just because you (or the previous owner of your house) planted a shrub or a tree in the wrong place doesn't mean it has to stay there forever.

Few of us are immune to the mad desire to hack away during our first forays into the garden. For example, at our first home, we tackled a 15' (4.5 m) apple tree while we were still clueless about pruning. We'd read that apples should be pruned in late winter, so my husband proceeded to saw off the top 3' (1 m) of growth all around. We'd just done the big no-no: topping a tree. Come spring, the tree frantically sprouted shoots to grow back branches and leaves it had lost, and it was much the same story the following spring too. To get rid of the rampant new growth, I spent an afternoon teetering precariously on the stepladder, vainly hoping to do a better job. Again a forest of shoots—called water sprouts, I was to learn—grew back.

The arborist I consulted said we must really hate the tree to treat it so badly. Actually, he was right: It wasn't a great tree, and it was growing in the middle of where we wanted a patio. The kindest cut would have been chopping it down. But like many starter gardeners, we assumed it could be cut into virtually any size or shape like a piece of lumber. Lesson learned. We removed the tree, got more space for the patio, and planted a proper shade tree in a better spot nearby (a katsura tree that is doing nicely, thank you).

Why prune?

The reasons for pruning are simple—to correct flawed form (branches that are growing badly or rubbing), to encourage better growth, to remove dead branches, and to thin out the canopy for more air and light. But pruning can't do what most people think it can: The height and shape of most trees and shrubs is determined by genetics. And the trouble with poor pruning is that it forces you into more pruning because your cuts stimulate growth. Yes, there are plants amenable to severe shaping—those used for hedges and topiaries—yews, privet, boxwood, and cedars, for example. But this is a high-maintenance game that most people reject in favor of a more carefree style of gardening.

Giving a shrub a facelift

Hard pruning to just above soil level encourages bushy new growth.

Thinning a shrub

Cut out the oldest, thickest stems to allow more sun into the interior of the plant.

Pruning out lower branches

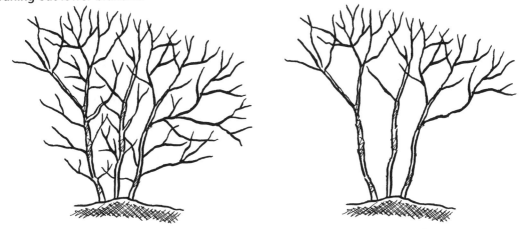

To create a more tree-like shrub, prune off lower side branches, leaving main upright stems.

The kindest cuts: Pruning rules for woody plants

- Make sure your pruning tools are sharp and clean. If you're pruning a diseased plant and you're worried about the chance of spreading a diseases or virus (yes, plants get viruses too), use a spray bottle filled with a solution of one part chlorine bleach or rubbing alcohol and 10 parts water. Spray your cutting tool and wipe it dry before moving to the next plant.
- Cut dead wood back to healthy growth.
- When cutting off part of a branch or a twig, always cut to an outward-facing bud to encourage new growth in that direction.
- When cutting off an entire branch, avoid leaving an unsightly stub. It won't callous over properly, and cracks and crevices will eventually form for diseases and insects to penetrate. Cut to the branch/bark ridge.
- Never top a tree—reduce its height by sawing limbs back—you'll ruin its natural form, encourage water sprouts, and create stress, leading to its decline.
- Never remove more than one third of live branches in one season.
- Don't prune in late summer or early fall; this promotes tender new growth that won't have enough time to harden off properly before winter.

When to prune trees

- Dead wood, or diseased or injured limbs: any time.
- Deciduous trees: in mid winter, when they're dormant. Wait about six to eight weeks after all their leaves have fallen. In winter, branching patterns are more obvious and cuts will heal quickly when new growth resumes. Winter pruning is especially beneficial for trees such as oaks that are susceptible to pests spreading serious diseases such as oak wilt if they're pruned during the growing season.
- Trees that "bleed" a lot of sap when pruned in spring, such as maple, dogwood, and birch: in winter. Don't panic if they bleed a little in spring—this is not a huge problem.
- Spring-flowering trees: right after they finish flowering.
- Summer-flowering trees: in late winter or early spring.
- Evergreens: in late spring or early summer.

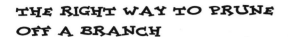

THE RIGHT WAY TO PRUNE OFF A BRANCH

When cutting off a branch, avoid cutting flush to the trunk. First, find what's called the branch bark collar, a slightly swollen growth where the branch comes out of the trunk. This area has special tissues that promote callusing to cover the wound and help the tree defend against disease and insects; it's vital that you not cut though it, even though a swollen knob is left in place. If this trunk collar has grown out on a dead limb to be removed, make the cut just beyond the collar. Don't cut into the collar.

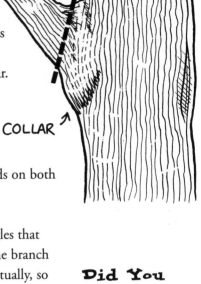

COLLAR →

Trees: What to prune away

- Suckers growing out of the base, so one strong main stem is left.
- Branches that cross and touch others. This creates wounds on both branches, and sometimes causes them to fuse together.
- Branches or twigs growing toward the center of the tree.
- Branches growing at sharp angles to the main trunk (angles that look like a sharp "V" at the crotch, the point at which the branch meets the trunk). These are more likely to break off eventually, so remove them in the first few years of growth.
- One of the limbs if two limbs are growing closer than 6" (15 cm) together. Between branches, aim for spacing of at least 12" to 16" (30 to 40 cm).
- Low-growing limbs. As the tree grows taller, branches don't move up, so a limb that extends out at a low point on the trunk will continue to grow out as the tree matures. Prune these away while the tree is young, but don't remove all the low-growing limbs at one time—stagger this pruning over several seasons, as these limbs help the trunk to grow strong.

Pruning young trees

By looking after a tree's "architecture" early, you'll promote sound, healthy growth and avoid expensive pruning to correct problems later on. Do a little pruning each year over the first three to four years so you never prune off too much at one time (remember, the more leaves, the more energy for growth).

Did You Know?

Tree wound dressings are out

Forget about painting a pruning wound. Tree wounds don't actually heal; instead, trees seal them off by developing callous tissue that gradually grows over the wound. Research shows that tree paint or wound dressings can contribute to decay by trapping moisture inside the cut. See? I saved you from another job.

Pruning mature trees: Not a do-it-yourself job

If your mature shade tree has a lot of dead branches and twigs, congested branching, or storm damage, it could use a trim to look first-rate again. Is the job large enough to require a ladder? Then bite the bullet and call an expert—ditto if it's located near power lines, your house, your neighbor's house, or the sidewalk. A qualified arborist (tree expert) has the training and equipment to prune a large tree correctly and safely. When interviewing arborists, ask if they have International Society of Arboriculture (ISA) certification or its local equivalent, which shows they have passed extensive exams and are up to date on all aspects of tree care.

And, by the way, a good pruning job looks subtle: The tree never screams out, *Hey, I've just been pruned.*

Pruning flowering shrubs

If you've chosen plants that suit your space, you need to do maintenance pruning to shape and rejuvenate flowering shrubs only every two years or so. A couple of pointers:

- Never shear flowering shrubs at the tips or they will become bare in the center and have fewer flowers. Do remove dead, injured, or

Pruning cuts

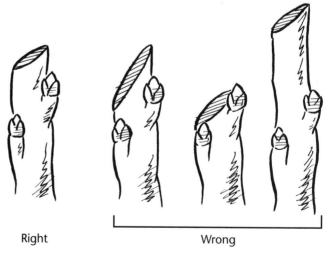

Right   Wrong

The correct cut is made at a 45-degree angle above an outward-facing bud.

diseased branches or twigs, those that rub against each other, and any that spoil the shrub's natural shape.

• Remove a few of the thickest and oldest stems, especially on shrubs that send numerous new stems out of the ground (this is called suckering). Do this every couple of years and your shrub continually renews itself. (If only we could stay shapely and young like this too!)

It's a jungle out there

So you've recently moved to a house and inherited a forest of dubious trees and shrubs—some scraggly, others overgrown and showing signs of pruning abuse. Don't despair. Here's a five-point game plan:

1. Find out what's what. If you're stuck, check out books, take branches and leaves to the garden center, or ask a knowledgeable friend or neighbor. Decide what's worth salvaging: Keep plants that look like they have the potential to grow gracefully.

2. Be ruthless. Every thin, scraggly, light-starved plant should be discarded, as should most self-sown seedling trees and shrubs that take over a neglected yard. If it doesn't look good, you can be sure it's *not* a horticultural treasure. Decide if any of the shrubs are worth keeping and moving to another spot in the garden. These plants can be dug up and relocated in spring before leafing out or mid-fall. (For the how-to, see box below.)

Moving shrubs and small trees

You'll need a spade or shovel and one or two sturdy pieces of burlap or tarp big enough for you and a helper to carry the plant. If it's dry, water the plant generously a day or two before moving it. To do the job:

• Dig a trenched circle around the plant. Make it wide enough to get a decent-sized root ball. You will have to use the spade to cut through woody roots.

• Cut under root ball with spade to free the plant. Then carefully work a piece of burlap under the root ball.

• If the soil is loose around the root ball, tie the burlap around to keep the root ball intact and use a second piece of burlap to put under the plant as a carrying sling. If the root ball is very heavy, hoist it into a cart or wheelbarrow. (You can skip tying up the root ball if it's quite firm—simply use the burlap to carry the plant. In clay soils, the root ball tends to stay intact, but it can easily fall apart in sandy soils.)

• Replant, water, and mulch. Keep moist until the plant is re-established in its new home.

---

3. Look critically at deciduous shrubs. If they're overgrown, or badly misshapen by shearing, you'll have to be cruel to be kind. Do a "hard pruning"—that means lopping off all stems to within 5" or 6" (12 to 15 cm) of the ground in late winter or early spring before growth starts. All right, there's a chance the plant could die, but in most cases, within a season or two it'll look good as new—certainly better than it does now.

4. If all the evergreen shrubs have been pruned into hamburger buns or tuna cans, consider letting them grow out into more natural shapes by not pruning them for a season or two.

5. Put a layer of mulch, compost, or chopped up leaves under keeper trees and shrubs—chances are they're starved for humus—and consider shade-tolerant ground covers planted underneath to unify them into a bed.

There. Doesn't that look better already? Now that you have things under control, regular maintenance pruning will keep your rejuvenated woody plants looking shipshape. What's more, if you're lucky, you will have created great spaces for your own (better) choices.

Feeling better? You're welcome.

What to do about stumps

Okay, you've cut some trees and shrubs down and now you're left with stumps. Here are your options:

• Elbow grease: This won't work for the really big ones, but if the stump is small enough and you have a strong back (or can bribe somebody who does), you should be able to dig it out with a pick and shovel. Make sure there are no buried hydro, gas, or telephone lines where you'll be working.

• Chemical removal: Garden centers sell products that are supposed to speed a stump's rotting. You drill holes in the wood and pour in the chemical, but then you'll have to be patient for several seasons. This is not a quick method.

• Hire a stump grinder: This is my preferred solution for large-sized stumps, as I like to leave a clean slate. These machines have blades that grind the stump to below ground level. This is a good method if the ground is level, with no buried rocks and—this is extremely important—no utility lines in the area. You can rent the machine or, better still (and safer for you), have a tree service do the job.

- If all this sounds like too much work or money, you could live with the stump. Try cutting it level with the ground, plunk a bird bath on top, and surround it with ground cover plants—or leave it higher and turn it into a plant stand or garden seat.

Up, up, and away: Climbing Vines

Many new gardeners are focused on the ground—after all that's where plants grow. But take a look up. There's something you can grow besides trees and shrubs that will add height, texture, and color to your garden: vines and climbing plants. I mentioned a few vines in Chapter 8, but there are plenty of hardy woody climbers you could invite to your garden party.

One of the best traits of vines is their ability to screen all the stuff you'd rather not see, like your messy neighbor's bits and pieces, your compost pile, a chain link fence, or an ugly garden shed or garage.

Since vines need to climb on something, all they ask is that you decide on what that something is. A trellis, an arbor, a rustic willow or elegant wrought iron support, a fence, or any number of structures can add style to your garden. Just remember to harmonize the support structure with your house and garden, and make sure it's sturdy enough. As with all plants, choose the right vine for your setting, sun lovers in sun, shady characters in shade, moist soil for a vine that requires it . . . and so on. (You know this by now, right?)

Most vines twine around support structures or hold fast to upright surfaces. For example, wisteria weaves or twines on a support, while climbing hydrangea and English or Boston ivy can attach to walls with aerial roots or adhesive pads. Then there are those that clasp with tendrils or petioles, such as clematis, or those with thorns that hook onto supports, such as climbing roses.

Fabulous flowering climbers

The following vines are another terrific way to add color to your garden.

- **Clematis:** Large-flowered clematis hybrids, hardy from zone 4 to 8, are deciduous vines that climb 8' to 12' (2.5 to 3.5 m) by twining stems and tendrils. Flowering time varies from late spring until frost, depending on the species or cultivar. Available in a profusion of flower colors (white, blue, violet, purple, pink and red or bicolor). Full sun or part shade and loamy, moist but well-drained soil. Pruning depends on variety: many cultivars bloom on the current season's growth and should be cut down almost to the ground in early spring just before new growth starts. Prune those that bloom on previous year's growth immediately after flowering. (Pruning information should be on your plant tag, so be sure to hold onto it until you get your clematis care routine down.)

- **Japanese wisteria** (*Wisteria floribunda*), **Chinese wisteria** (*Wisteria sinensis*): Vigorous twining vines, hardy from zone 5 to 9, growing to 25' or 30' (7.5 to 9 m). Both types are loved for long dangling clusters of fragrant blue flowers in spring and have strong woody stems that need a sturdy support posts (the flowers of the Japanese type are longer than those of the Chinese type). Wisteria grows best in moist, well-drained soil in full sun. Do a midsummer pruning of new growth back to about 6" (15 cm) of main stems and prune shoots again in late winter back to two or three buds.

- **Climbing roses** (*Rosa*): The term "climbing roses" is a tad misleading. Roses don't climb the way that vines like clematis or wisteria do. They are simply rose varieties with long, arching canes (the rose fancier's word for stem) that can grow about 10' (3 m) tall. Left to their own devices, such roses grow into big, unmanageable shrubs, hooking their thorns into anything around, including unwary gardeners. But you can get them to climb by tying the canes to a support post or latticed trellis, (a cuss-inducing job best done wearing long sleeves and leather gloves to protect from the thorns).

  Canadian rose breeders have developed hardy shrub roses named after famous explorers. Of this group, the following make good climbers: 'John Cabot,' with its fragrant red double flowers; 'Martin Frobisher,' with fragrant light pink flowers; and 'William Baffin,' with deep pink, double flowers that aren't scented. These cultivars are hardy from zone 3 to 10 and need full sun.

Don't have full sun?

Don't worry: Few climbing vines thrive in the dark, but the following do well in light shade as well as in sun:

- **Boston ivy, Virginia creeper (*Parthenocissus* species):** Both are deciduous climbers that turn red in fall. Virginia creeper (*Parthenocissus quinquefolia*), zone 3 to 9, is extremely vigorous and grows 10' (3 m) a year when established. Grows 30' to 50' (9 to 15 m), as does Boston ivy (*Parthenocissus tricuspidata*), zone 4 to 8. Both are self-clinging with suction-cup holdfasts, but Boston ivy is a less rampant grower than Virginia creeper.
- **Climbing hydrangea (*Hydrangea anomala* subspecies *petiolaris*):** Deciduous vine with attractive clusters of large white flowers in midsummer. Roots produced on stems attach plant to supports. Hardy from zone 4 to 8, it is slow to establish, but will grow 25' (7.5 m) or more.
- **Five-leaf akebia (*Akebia quinata*):** Fast-growing deciduous twining vine, zones 5 to 8, with attractive glossy leaves and small purple flowers in mid spring. Makes a terrific screen and will grow 30' to 40' (9 to 12 m).

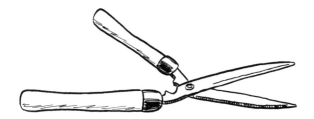

Chapter 11

Taste Buds: Growing Good Stuff to Eat

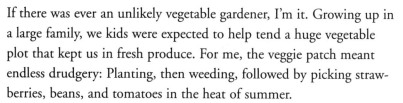

If there was ever an unlikely vegetable gardener, I'm it. Growing up in a large family, we kids were expected to help tend a huge vegetable plot that kept us in fresh produce. For me, the veggie patch meant endless drudgery: Planting, then weeding, followed by picking strawberries, beans, and tomatoes in the heat of summer.

These days, I have my own vegetable garden (not as large, thank goodness), and to my mother's amusement, it brings me almost as much pleasure as my flower garden. There's something special about eating from the garden. Fresh-picked peas are a revelation—store-bought ones never tasted as sweet—and who can resist juicy, garden-ripe tomatoes still warm from the sun? At the dinner table, I love announcing that the makings of the pasta sauce—the tomatoes, onions, peppers, garlic, and herbs—all came from the garden. In addition, I grow other easy favorites—asparagus and rhubarb (both perennials), salad greens, beans, peas, peppers, and summer squash, including the dreaded zucchini. With the exception of tomatoes,

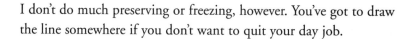

I don't do much preserving or freezing, however. You've got to draw the line somewhere if you don't want to quit your day job.

KISS Your Veggie Patch

The key to enjoying a vegetable garden? Keep It Simple, Stupid! Grow only what you like to eat. Your family hates zucchini? Forget it. Here are a few things to consider:

- Grow the stuff you have to shell out bigger bucks for at the super-market—that means specialty greens like arugula or mesclun salad mixes, or asparagus. In fact, asparagus is one of the few vegetables that's perennial. For a Saturday spent planting your patch, you can harvest for 12 to 15 years. Honest! (See page 130 for the how-to.)
- Other homegrown crops that are noticeably tastier and cheaper include green and yellow beans, broccoli, Brussels sprouts, carrots, green onions, leeks, peas (both shelling and snow types), peppers, spinach, tomatoes, and zucchini.
- Grow what's not so readily available. Many varieties for home gardeners aren't found in stores, because produce intended for shipping is bred for durability and shelf life—taste comes a distant second. That's why many flavorful old and heirloom varieties are making a comeback. Most of these you'll have to start from seed, which isn't that hard to do on a sunny windowsill or under grow lights if you follow the instructions on the seed packet, or by planting straight out into the garden when appropriate.

Veggie Garden Basics

Choose a level, well-drained spot that gets at least eight hours of full sun each day, and make sure it's near a water source. The closer to the house, the easier the plants are to tend. Vegetables love rich soil, so improve the soil first by working in compost or manure. (Refer back to chapter 3 for all the dirty details.) Plant taller crops on the north side so low-growing ones won't get shaded out. More tips:

- Start small. Starter gardeners often overplant and become over-whelmed. You don't even need a separate vegetable garden to begin with. Try tucking a tomato plant or two into your patch of annuals—each plant will need a space 3' square (just under a square meter)—or plant basil, parsley, thyme, and chives in a half-barrel planter near the kitchen door or use them as edging plants in the flower bed.

• If you want a separate vegetable garden, it doesn't have to be big. I'm amazed at how many plants I can grow in one of my rectangular 10' by 20' (3 meters by 6 meters) vegetable beds. To make it look pretty, I edge the bed with parsley alternating with 'Orange Gem' marigolds or calendulas (pot marigolds).

Seeds or plants?

Many vegetables—beans, peas, carrots, corn, lettuce, and spinach—grow best if seeded directly into the soil. How deep you plant them depends on the size of the seed. A good general rule is to plant three times as deep as the diameter of the seed. Very fine seeds are barely covered, while large seeds, such as beans or peas, go deeper. Seed packets usually have planting instructions —how deep and how far apart to plant—and information on how many days the seeds will take to germinate and number of days until harvest.

Tiny seeds such as carrots and lettuce are hard to plant a specific distance apart, so you have to remove excess seedlings (a process called thinning). It's hard to force yourself to pull out tiny living plants you actually grew from seed, but if the seed packet recommends thinning, do it; otherwise, your plants will be crowded and they won't develop properly.

Garden centers sell young vegetable plants (called transplants) for such popular crops as tomatoes, cabbage, broccoli, cauliflower, and peppers. You could grow these from seed yourself, but in the first season it's easier to buy transplants. (The main reason for starting your own seedlings is to try varieties not readily available at garden centers.) The easiest way to grow onions is to buy tiny bulb onions called onion sets, which you plant quite shallowly, so a bit of their neck still shows.

Some like it hot

You don't have to wait until the frost-free date in the spring to start planting vegetables. Some like it cool and grow best before the heat of summer really gets going; others like it hot and those you plant later.

- Cool customers include greens (lettuce, spinach, arugula, mesclun salad mixes, Swiss chard), the cabbage clan (cabbage, broccoli, cauliflower), and peas (shelling, sugar snap, and snow types). They relish temperatures between 60°F and the low 70s (16°C to 22°C), but bolt into flower and go to seed quickly when temperatures soar above the mid-80s (above 30°C). Plant these crops when the earliest daffodils bloom.

- Heat-seeking crops—tomatoes, eggplant, peppers, corn, squash, zucchini, cucumbers, and beans—are happiest when both the soil and air temperatures average 60°F (16°C) and above, day and night. Plant these when the soil has warmed up and there is no more chance of frost, generally in late May or into early June, or whatever the frost-free date is in your region.

Avoiding the Dreaded Zucchini Syndrome

Your kids sneak out the back door come dinner time, your neighbors won't answer the door—nobody can cope with another zucchini from your garden.

If you haven't grown vegetables before, you'll be amazed at how prolific they can be. To avoid too much of a good thing, plant small quantities (suggested quantities for today's smaller families follow). Never plant the entire contents of a packet containing more than 10 seeds. The excess seed will keep until next year if stored in a cool, dry place. And remember: *Nobody's expecting you to grow everything on the list.* Your first time out, just pick several favorites you'd like to try.

- Beans, green or yellow bush type: one 4' (1.2 m) row. Pole beans: one teepee, made of three bamboo stakes tied together at the top with about three seeds planted at the base of each pole; or string the teepees and plant along the sides of the triangle. Pole beans are great for limited space—they produce over a longer period of time, while bush beans yield only one crop.
- Cabbage, cauliflower, broccoli: two or four plants of each kind (they generally all ripen at the same time).
- Carrots: one or two 4' (1.2 m) rows.
- Corn: a dozen plants arranged in a square block (corn is wind-pollinated, so if you grow it in a single row, pollination is reduced. And no pollination = no corn).
- Lettuce and greens such as spinach: one 2' to 4" (60 cm to 1.2 m) row of each kind.
- Peas, shelling or snow types: one 8' (2.5 m) row.
- Peppers: six to eight plants. Try one or two plants of three or four different varieties.
- Potatoes: 12 plants.
- Tomatoes: three or four plants of one or two varieties.
- Zucchini and other summer squashes: one plant (or two, if you want to live dangerously), and don't try more than a couple of varieties (they grow prolifically, so consider yourself warned!).

Tips on Harvesting

One of the joys of vegetable gardening is freshness, so harvest just before you want to eat the vegetable and pick crops while they're on the young and tender side and not overripe. Remember to:

- Walk through your garden every day and pick ripe fruit and vegetables. Keeping your crops harvested encourages many plants to continue producing longer.
- If a vegetable is overripe or otherwise unfit to eat, add it to your compost heap.

You Say Tomato...

If you grow just a few edibles, I'll bet tomatoes are at the top of your list. There are many types to choose from: small, sweet cherry types (lovely in salads and roasted), medium-sized and beefsteaks (both great for sandwiches), and plum types (which make terrific sauces). And you'll find them in different colors—from glossy red to pink to yellow—and shapes. 'Yellow Pear' is a cherry variety I'm especially fond of.

Another consideration is growth habit. Some tomato plants, called "determinate," grow to a certain height and then stop. These are generally preferred for canning because they flower and set all their fruit within a short period. But most home gardeners prefer "indeterminate" types—varieties that grow, flower, and set fruit over a much longer period, stopping only when the weather gets too cold. The plant tag will usually tell you what kind you're getting.

Planting

Buy healthy young plants with dark green leaves—avoid ones with fruit and flowers already on them. Tomatoes are particularly sensitive to low night temperatures in late spring: They'll lose their blossoms if temperatures fall below 55°F (12.8°C), so don't plant until frost is well gone. Besides warm weather, tomatoes need full sun and plenty of water. Set your plants about 30" (75 cm) apart.

Staking

Most tomatoes benefit from staking; otherwise, they'll sprawl all over the garden. Another reason to support stems is to keep fruit off the ground, where it's likely to rot or be attacked by insects. You can tie plants to a single stake or—even easier—put a tomato cage (readily available at most garden centers) around them. Put the cage in place when you plant—getting it over a mature plant is next to impossible.

Care

Tomatoes do best with a steady supply of moisture. If plants seesaw between drying out and heavy watering, the skin splits. Check plants regularly for little side shoots in the leaf axils (where the leaf comes off the main stem) and pinch them out with your fingers when they're about 1" (2.5 cm) long.

Troubleshooting

What can go wrong with tomatoes?

- Blight: In cool, wet summers tomatoes can get blight, a fungal disease that causes leaves and stems to turn brown. Prune affected leaves off the plant and avoid planting tomatoes in the same spot next year. (In fact, this is a good idea with all your vegetables. Rotate them around your veggie patch instead of planting them in the same place each season.)
- Blossom-end rot: This causes the bottoms of tomatoes to turn brown or blackish, and results from a lack of calcium in the soil or irregular watering. Prevention: Feed plants with a tomato fertilizer containing calcium and keep plants well watered, never allowing them to dry out.
- Tomato hornworms: I'd grown tomatoes for several years before stumbling across these guys. They're hard to spot (they're as green as and as thick as a tomato stem, a very clever camouflage), but once you notice them, you'll be amazed at their size—about as thick as your finger or thumb. Yuck! Handpicking is a very effective control, so get your gloves (or your kitchen tongs) out and pick them off whenever you see them; otherwise, they'll eat your tomatoes and plants right to the ground. (If you can't bring yourself to stomp on them, drown them in a pail of soapy water.) A week to 10 days of vigilance and you'll solve the problem. Some gardeners swear by growing lots of dill nearby—hornworms also like dill and are easier to spot on dill plants.

Want Your Own Asparagus Patch?

Asparagus is a perennial veggie that commands high prices in the supermarket. If you love these tender green spears and you're planning to stay put for a while, planting a patch is definitely worth it—you'll be harvesting it for years. (It was one of the first things I did after we were settled into our new garden.)

Plant in mid spring at the north side of the garden so other plants won't get shaded. About 16 to 20 plants will be enough for a small family. Don't use seed; buy crowns (the root system of a one-year-old plant) of male varieties such as Jersey Giant, Jersey Prince, or Jersey Knight. (Female plants expend energy to produce seeds, which decreases the number of spears produced.)

Here's the how-to:

- Dig a furrow about 6" (15 cm) deep. Old-timers recommend planting twice as deep, but new research shows that fewer spears are produced with deeper planting. Set crowns 18" (46 cm) apart and rows 3' to 4' (about 1 m) apart.
- After planting, fill the furrow to its original soil level. Don't pack soil down too hard or you might injure the buds of emerging spears. Spears should show within a week or two.
- Asparagus is drought-tolerant but will need extra watering during the first couple of months if there isn't enough rain. Mulch with a 3" (7.5 cm) layer of straw.
- In fall, after the ferny foliage turns yellow and brittle, cut it back and, to keep the bed fertile, spread a layer of compost or well-rotted manure at least 1" (2.5 cm) thick over the bed. Finish off with a new layer of straw about 3" (7.5 cm) thick.
- Keep the bed weed-free for years of edible pleasure from your patch.

This next bit of information will put off the instant-gratification crowd, but aren't good things worth waiting for? Since they're going to be in place for years, asparagus plants need two growing seasons to get established. Those first tempting spears have to open up into ferny leaves that produce the food the plants need to get their strength up and running.

For picking, follow the 2-4-8 rule: Pick for two weeks in the third year, then four weeks in the fourth year, and eight weeks in subsequent years. Just snap off the upper 7" to 10" (18 to 25 cm) tender green portion. Harvest all spears that come up during the harvest period and then allow the rest to leaf out.

Spice Up Your Garden with Herbs

Why not grow a few herbs to add taste and zest to your cooking? Many herbs make an attractive addition to your veggie garden. You can even tuck them into a sunny flowerbed, where they'll happily keep company with annuals and perennials. Lavender, for example, is gorgeous as a front-of-the-bed edging plant.

Many herbs thrive with little care, and because they hail from Mediterranean regions, they tend to flourish in heat, dryness, and sun. Even better, they have few insect and disease problems and grow well in average garden soil.

Here's what you'll need to know to get started:

- Herbs need well-drained soil and full sun (six hours daily). Like most plants, they need watering to get established and should be watered if you're experiencing a prolonged drought.
- Some herbs, such as dill and cilantro, are annuals. Harvest these two to three months after sowing from seed (you can buy annual herbs as seedling plants, but they are easy to grow from seed, and you'll get stronger, healthier plants that way). Annual herbs tend to flower and go to seed quickly. When that happens, their leaves lose flavor, so for a fresh supply, some gardeners sow a little more seed two or three times over the summer so they can stagger their harvest over the season. To harvest, snip off leaves or pull the entire plant.
- Like perennial flowers, perennial herbs such as French tarragon, sage, and thyme will come back year after year. When starting out, buy small plants. (You can grow many perennial herbs from seed, but it takes a season or two for them to get big enough to harvest.)
- Allow perennial herbs six to eight weeks of growth before harvesting. Avoid removing too many leaves or stems at one time—remember, plants need plenty of leaves to thrive. To harvest, snip a piece of stem with sharp scissors, pruners, or a knife. Never tear stems off—you might injure or even pull out the roots. Once herbs are established, regular pruning promotes lush new growth, which has the best flavor.

Try growing herbs in containers

This is a great way to have kitchen herbs at hand or to grow them if you don't have oodles of space. Mint is one herb best grown in a pot—left to its own exuberant devices, it can easily stage a coup in the garden. Another good container herb is rosemary, a tough woody perennial in warmer climates, but not hardy in cold northern winters. Growing herbs in pots makes it easier to take them inside for the cold months.

To be successful in pots, herbs need:

- Containers about 10" to 12" (25 to 30 cm) deep, with one or more holes for good drainage, and soil-less potting mix.
- Full sun for a minimum of six hours a day.
- Water: Many herbs will tolerate drier conditions than other container plants. How much to water depends on the weather, the plants, and the size and type of pot. Terra cotta containers dry out quickly and often need daily watering in high summer. The larger the pot, the easier it is to keep moist.
- Fertilizer: Slow-release fertilizer pellets added to the top layer of potting mix at planting will feed your herbs throughout the growing season. Alternatively, use soluble fertilizer once a week when watering.

Keeping herbs indoors over the winter

It's tempting to take container-grown herbs, especially perennial types, inside for the winter.

Unfortunately, during northern winters even a south-facing window gets a lot less sun than the plants need, and central heating makes the air very dry. Remember, these plants thrive in the Mediterranean, where the summers are hot and winters are brighter and moist. Your herbs won't be as flavorful in winter: They need heat and sun to create the aromatic oils that keep them zesty.

If you're still keen to try,

- In early fall, move containers to a semi-shaded spot outdoors to get herbs used to lower light levels.
- When taking them indoors, set pots in a sunny south-facing window and add a florescent grow light for extra brightness.
- Water when potting soil feels dry to touch, and mist frequently.
- Growth will slow down, so harvest only small amounts if your goal is to keep plants for next year. Otherwise, keep harvesting until you use up the leaves, then toss the plant.

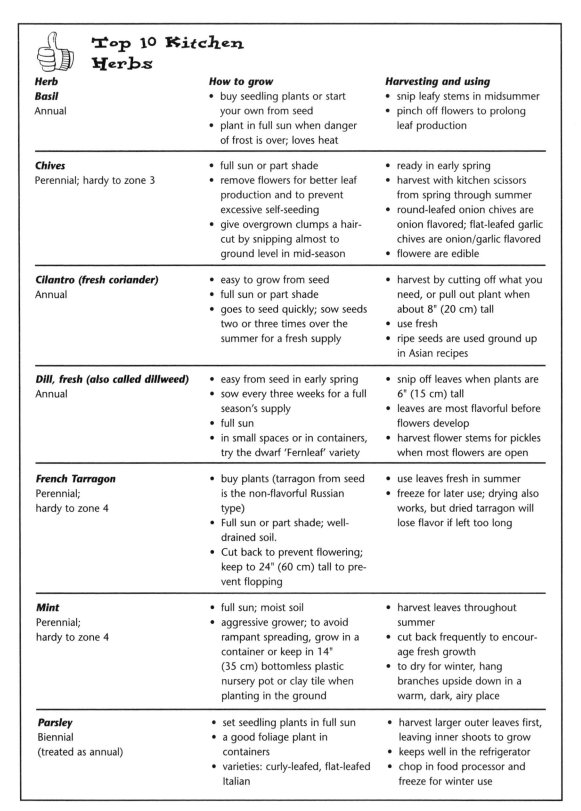

Top 10 Kitchen Herbs

Herb	How to grow	Harvesting and using
Basil Annual	• buy seedling plants or start your own from seed • plant in full sun when danger of frost is over; loves heat	• snip leafy stems in midsummer • pinch off flowers to prolong leaf production
Chives Perennial; hardy to zone 3	• full sun or part shade • remove flowers for better leaf production and to prevent excessive self-seeding • give overgrown clumps a haircut by snipping almost to ground level in mid-season	• ready in early spring • harvest with kitchen scissors from spring through summer • round-leafed onion chives are onion flavored; flat-leafed garlic chives are onion/garlic flavored • flowere are edible
Cilantro (fresh coriander) Annual	• easy to grow from seed • full sun or part shade • goes to seed quickly; sow seeds two or three times over the summer for a fresh supply	• harvest by cutting off what you need, or pull out plant when about 8" (20 cm) tall • use fresh • ripe seeds are used ground up in Asian recipes
Dill, fresh (also called dillweed) Annual	• easy from seed in early spring • sow every three weeks for a full season's supply • full sun • in small spaces or in containers, try the dwarf 'Fernleaf' variety	• snip off leaves when plants are 6" (15 cm) tall • leaves are most flavorful before flowers develop • harvest flower stems for pickles when most flowers are open
French Tarragon Perennial; hardy to zone 4	• buy plants (tarragon from seed is the non-flavorful Russian type) • Full sun or part shade; well-drained soil. • Cut back to prevent flowering; keep to 24" (60 cm) tall to prevent flopping	• use leaves fresh in summer • freeze for later use; drying also works, but dried tarragon will lose flavor if left too long
Mint Perennial; hardy to zone 4	• full sun; moist soil • aggressive grower; to avoid rampant spreading, grow in a container or keep in 14" (35 cm) bottomless plastic nursery pot or clay tile when planting in the ground	• harvest leaves throughout summer • cut back frequently to encourage fresh growth • to dry for winter, hang branches upside down in a warm, dark, airy place
Parsley Biennial (treated as annual)	• set seedling plants in full sun • a good foliage plant in containers • varieties: curly-leafed, flat-leafed Italian	• harvest larger outer leaves first, leaving inner shoots to grow • keeps well in the refrigerator • chop in food processor and freeze for winter use

Top 10 Kitchen Herbs (continued)

Herb	How to grow	Harvesting and using
Rosemary Perennial; hardy to zone 7 with winter mulch	• full sun • not winter-hardy in most northern regions, but terrific in containers • a bright, unheated sun porch works for winter if temperatures don't dip below −21°F (6°C)	• to harvest, snip tender stem tips; new growth will branch out from cuts. • dries well: hang in bunches in a dry, dark, airy spot
Sage Perennial; hardy to zone 5	• full sun; moist but well-drained soil. • plants may lose vigor after a few seasons; dig up and replace with new ones	• pick leaves over summer, but harvest sparingly in the first season when it's getting established • easy to dry: hang branches in a dry, dark, airy spot
Thyme Perennial; hardy to zone 4	• full sun; well-drained soil • in very cold winter areas, mulch with light layer of pine needles after ground freezes • trim in early spring to remove brown stems and winter dieback	• snip leaves and sprigs all summer • dries well: tie several sprigs together and hang upside down in a warm, dark, airy place

Chapter 12

Pot Luck: The Joy of Container Gardening

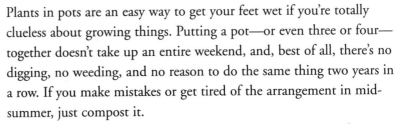

Plants in pots are an easy way to get your feet wet if you're totally clueless about growing things. Putting a pot—or even three or four—together doesn't take up an entire weekend, and, best of all, there's no digging, no weeding, and no reason to do the same thing two years in a row. If you make mistakes or get tired of the arrangement in mid-summer, just compost it.

Decks, patios, outdoor steps, balconies, rooftops—any surface, even a driveway—can be transformed into a lush display of stuff you actually grew, so read on for the basics of pot culture (well, not *that* kind). But promise you won't do the ubiquitous ring of red geraniums around a spiky dracaena. That combo has been a container cliché for as long as anyone can remember, and you're far more creative than that—aren't you?

Choosing Containers: Au Natural Is Best

The secret to success is getting containers—pots, window boxes, and hanging baskets—of a decent size. You don't want your containers to fade into the background like wallflowers at the prom—the great outdoors demands bigger gestures. The larger they are, the more space for plants and their roots, the more interesting your combinations, and the less you'll be a slave to the hose.

Garden centers will tempt you to buy pricey instant container gardens already potted up, generally in cheap plastic pots. This is container gardening at its most idiot-proof. If you can't resist, at least stick the arrangement, plastic pot and all, into a nicer pot when you get home. The most popular containers are made of terra cotta, wood, or plastic. Natural materials win hands down over plastic when it comes to looks—and in gardening, looks matter. As well, roots need oxygen, so porous materials such as clay or wood are better in that department too.

Terra cotta—clay—pots are affordable and available in many classic shapes and sizes. Terra cotta isn't frost-proof, however, so after the summer show, empty and wash pots and store in the basement. If you love color, glazed ceramic pots suit bold displays, but they too are not frost-proof.

Molded polyethylene pots are recent additions to the container scene. Frost-proof, and only about 10% of the weight of clay pots, the best versions recreate classic shapes and look remarkably authentic—you have to touch them or lift them to figure out that they're not the real thing. Unfortunately, they're pricier than terra cotta. They're also not as porous, so you need to pay extra attention to drainage. Stand the pot on a couple of bricks or something similar so excess water can drain out quickly.

Wooden containers—window boxes and halved whiskey barrels—are easy to find. If you're planning a window box, it should be at least 8" to 10" (20 to 25 cm) wide and deep; anything smaller is hard to keep moist in hot weather. Remember that a wooden box, plus moist soil and plants, is a weighty thing and mount it with properly anchored supports. On high-rise balconies, place window boxes inside the railing to minimize the risk of dropping a watering can or the

Retired objects can make a second debut as spontaneous containers. The sky is the limit—watering cans, wicker baskets, sap buckets, clay pipes or hollow logs can all be pressed into service. The bigger, the better—and if it doesn't drain well, drill several drainage holes.

whole box to the ground. (What's funny in Bugs Bunny cartoons isn't so funny in real life.) Wood isn't forever, but lining the interior with a sheet of plastic and giving the container a coat of stain will help extend its life, as will emptying it out over the winter.

Don't even think plastic for hanging plants. The most attractive choice is a large wire basket lined with a thick layer of sphagnum moss, which does a good job of insulating roots. Other liners, such as coir (made of coconut fiber), are also available. To improve the moisture-holding capacity, line the inside with an aluminum pie plate. (Because the basket lining is so free-draining, you don't need to poke drainage holes in the pie plate.)

Another durable material often used to make replicas of classic urns is concrete. If you're creative, a faux finish on your planter can turn it into an instant antique.

Spice Up Your Planting

The most interesting displays use several different plants arranged together. Many plants beyond the annuals commonly used will work well in containers. Today, lush tropicals such as passion flower, mandevilla, and jasmine vine, and even perennials such as ornamental grasses, hostas, and the interesting new heuchera hybrids, grown for their chocolate- or pewter-colored foliage, are making their way into planters.

As with all gardening, choose plants that suit your conditions of sun or shade. For example, herbs are just the thing for containers that bake in the sun. In a large terra cotta pot, try citrus-scented lemon gem marigolds around an aromatic Mediterranean herb or two—lavender, rosemary, sage—and then tuck in trailing nasturtiums. Fleshy-leaved hens and chicks (*Sempervivium*) or echevarias make fabulous drought-resistant plantings for folks who forget to water.

The Container Plant Hit List

The best container plants can weather heat waves, high humidity, and downpours. It's a tall order, but there are plants that fit the bill. Here's an easy container recipe: Choose one or two plants from the first column and fill in with plants from the trailing and foliage categories.

The number of plants depends on the container's size. To match plants to your light conditions, look under sun and shade categories. Three pointers:

- Use color themes from the house and surrounding garden plants.
- Don't throw in a bit of everything. Limit your choices to two or three colors that complement each other and add some interesting foliage to set the flowers off nicely. Foliage can echo the other colors or contrast with them.
- Group containers together to help them stay cooler and make watering easier. This gives you a chance to arrange them into an attractive "potscape."

Sun to semi-shade

Feature plants	Trailing or filler plants	Foliage plants
African daisy (*Osteospermum*)	Bacopa	Red Fountain grass (*Pennisetum setaceum* 'Rubrum')
Flowering maple (*Abutilon*)	Bidens "Goldmarie"	Sage: variegated or tri-colored
Geranium	Million Bells (*Calibracoa*)	Swedish ivy
Marguerite daisy	Petunias: Wave series or Surfinia	Sweet potato vine

Shade-tolerant

Feature plants	Trailing or filler plants	Foliage plants
Tuberous and wax begonias	Trailing verbena	Creeping Jenny
Hosta	Impatiens	English ivy
Coleus	Ivy geraniums	Licorice plant (*Helichrysum petiolare*): silver, lime-green, or variegated
Fuchsia	Blue fan flower (*Scaevola*)	Trailing vinca vine (*Vinca major* 'Variegata')

No Soil?

Real garden soil is a no-no for containers. It's full of weed seeds and gets so hard and dense in containers that it won't absorb moisture. The stuff to get is "soil-less" mix.

That's right: Potting mixes for containers don't contain any real soil at all—they're made of lightweight peat moss with additives for aeration and water absorption. If the mixture is dry when you open the bag, moisten it in a bucket and let it stand an hour or so before using.

Potting soil doesn't contain a lot of plant nutrients, so I like to supplement it with some added humus, either bagged manure or homemade compost. I aim for a mix that's two thirds potting soil to one third humus.

Ready, Set, Plant

First, assemble everything you need—plants, containers, potting mix, fertilizer—and work close to an outdoor faucet. You're often told to put pottery shards at the bottom of the container for drainage when planting, but it's the holes that actually provide drainage—you don't need the extra shards. If you're concerned about the planting mix leaking out, use a piece of broken pottery or a small stone over the drainage hole. I like to use screening mesh—the kind you buy in a roll to repair a screen door—cut in pieces large enough to cover the holes.

Next, fill your container about three quarters full with moist potting mix (keep it fluffy). Then remove plants from pots, gently tease roots apart if they're root-bound, and place the plants inside the container. Fill gaps between plants with more potting mix, firming it down gently to get rid of air pockets. Add a slow-release all-season fertilizer (see box below) following package directions. (It's usually mixed into the top layer of potting soil.)

Fertilizer in one easy step

Container plants must be fertilized regularly because you're asking a lot—masses of flowers in a tight space. But you're too busy to fertilize containers weekly, right?

Here's the easy solution: Before filling in around the plants with growing mix, add fertilizer pellets especially formulated to feed container plants for the entire season. Basically, these are slow-release fertilizers covered with a special coating so they release nutrients when temperature and moisture conditions are right and last all season long. For the amount to use, follow package directions.

Plant generously, but don't crowd your plants—they need space to grow. A pot 12" to 15" (30 to 38 cm) in diameter can take one to three plants, depending on their eventual size, and one double that size can take five or six plants. Avoid packing soil mix right up to the container's rim; leave 2" (5 cm) of space as a reservoir for easier watering. Then give your pot a generous watering.

$ When planting up a large, deep container, don't be alarmed by the amount of potting soil it can hold. To save on the mix, place a plastic nursery pot upside down inside the container and then add your potting soil.

Keeping Them Growing

Once you've planted your containers, watering is job one. Check containers daily and always water thoroughly until water comes out through the drainage hole. (Even when it rains, moisture may not penetrate further than a couple of inches into the pot.) Rather than hauling a watering can around, use a hose-end watering wand to provide a soft but thorough spray of water.

If you applied slow-release fertilizer when planting, pat yourself on the back. If you didn't, use an all-purpose fertilizer such as 20-20-20 dissolved in a watering can and water it in once a week, following product directions. Plants in containers depend on fertilizer, but they respond better to low, regular doses of fertilizer than to whacking amounts at one time.

When you're watering, check for finished flowers, deadhead (there's that menacing word again), and pinch off yellowed or dried up leaves.

To Keep or Not to Keep?

All good things come to an end, so what should you do with your container plants as cold weather approaches? The instructions for keeping plants over the winter are often involved and intimidating. "Who, me, take cuttings? You've got to be kidding," I hear you say. You may get there one day, but for now, let's keep it simple.

Annuals are easy—their remains go into the compost—and you can plant hardy perennials into a garden bed in early to mid fall, but what about longer-lived plants that aren't hardy in your region? You can try growing them under lights, but there's a risk of bringing insect pests inside (check plants over carefully beforehand, looking for

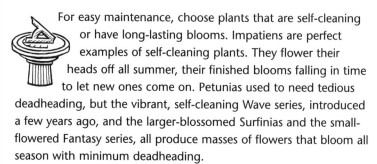

For easy maintenance, choose plants that are self-cleaning or have long-lasting blooms. Impatiens are perfect examples of self-cleaning plants. They flower their heads off all summer, their finished blooms falling in time to let new ones come on. Petunias used to need tedious deadheading, but the vibrant, self-cleaning Wave series, introduced a few years ago, and the larger-blossomed Surfinias and the small-flowered Fantasy series, all produce masses of flowers that bloom all season with minimum deadheading.

Other time-saving plants that clean up after themselves are the Tapien verbena series, which make great trailing plants in containers; Million Bells, a *Calibracoa* genus that looks like a tiny petunia; and *Bidens ferulifolia*, a cheerful yellow-flowered hanging plant sold under the name 'Goldmarie.' These and many more annuals have been introduced under the trade name Proven Winners. *Hint:* For easy-care annuals, the label may often say that the plant flowers generously "without pruning or pinching."

insects under the leaves). Indoor light over the winter tends to be too dim and the air inside our houses too hot and dry, so the results may be less than spectacular.

But with container gardening, as with all gardening, the consolation is: there's always next year.

Chapter 13

The Yuck Factor: Weeds, Pests, and Diseases

I try, but I have to admit I'm not a 100% organic gardener. But, these days, if I have an insect problem, spraying it with something that ends in "cide" is at the bottom of the list. I'll try other alternatives first—but when all else fails, I've been known to fall off the wagon.

There's no doubt that environmental concerns are changing the way we garden. In the past 25 years, we've come to realize that the quick fixes promised by pesticides and commercial fertilizers are no substitute for such good gardening practices as composting, mulching, adding humus to the soil, and choosing plants suited to our growing conditions. With mounting opposition to pesticide use and the current phase-out of many such products, we have more incentive than ever to take care of our gardens and back yards more naturally.

That being said, gardening still sometimes means making hard choices where you have to weigh the risks against the potential benefits of using a tough medicine. When a prized tree is in danger from a

> ## What is organic gardening anyway?
>
> The simple answer is that organic gardeners don't use manufactured or synthetic fertilizers or pesticides, but it's much more than that. Organic gardeners try to work within natural systems and they continually replenish the soil's humus. Organic gardening actually begins with attention to the soil (all that stuff you read about in Chapter 3) and strives to create a garden environment that's healthy and diverse.

serious pest, I weigh the long-term environmental benefits the tree will provide over the years against the short-term pain of spraying it. I research the problem to make sure I choose the right solution and don't just spray in the dark, so to speak. And if certain plants are repeatedly problematic, I stop growing them.

This chapter will cover the problems that can arise—weeds, insects, diseases, and four-legged critters that eat your plants—and suggest the most environmentally friendly ways of coping with what can go wrong.

Weedy Matters

My dictionary defines a weed as "a plant that is not valued where it is growing and is usually of vigorous growth; especially, one that tends to overgrow or choke out more desirable plants."

We could just say that if it grows like a weed, it generally *is* a weed—but what's a weed to you may not necessarily be a weed for me. For you, goldenrod may be a weed, but I've invited several nicely behaved ones into my perennial gardens, and in the less manicured parts of my property, I encourage native wild species.

You might think of weeds as intolerable vegetation invented by capricious nature to drive gardeners crazy. Not so—it's just that nature doesn't like soil straight up; she prefers it covered with greenery and has an arsenal of opportunistic plants precisely suited to this job.

Ever heard the old saying "One year's seeding equals seven years' weeding"? Well, it's true. A solitary plant of lamb's quarters, a common garden weed, can produce up to 70,000 seeds in one season, and

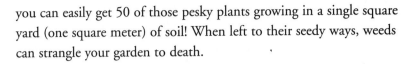

you can easily get 50 of those pesky plants growing in a single square yard (one square meter) of soil! When left to their seedy ways, weeds can strangle your garden to death.

Weed facts

- Annual weeds come in two forms: summer and winter annuals. Summer annuals such as lamb's quarters sprout in spring and go to seed in late summer and fall, but winter annuals such as chickweed sprout in fall, live over winter, and go to seed in spring or summer.
- Biennial weeds such as Queen Anne's lace and burdock form roots and a rosette of leaves the first year, then flower and set seed the second year.
- Perennial weeds such as quack grass and creeping Charlie live for more than two years and reproduce not only by seed, but also by stolons, roots, and stems. They're tough to eradicate because they can easily start to grow again from a small piece of root or stem.

Who's who in the garden?

Any plant growing in the wrong place can be a weed. Think of Norway maple seedlings in your hedge, or lawn grass that's crept into the flower bed. Weeds can make your garden look uncared for, and they compete with flowers and landscape plants for space, moisture, sunlight, and nutrients. Because they are tough and fast-growing, weeds can easily out-compete desirable plants if you don't take charge.

The first step is actually telling weeds and garden plants apart, especially in early spring, when they look pretty much the same to the

---

DID YOU KNOW?
Cultivation encourages weeds

Some seeds are viable for a year or two, but others can lie dormant for decades, waiting for a chance to grow. When they're buried several inches deep, there isn't enough light for germination—but if you work the soil and bring them to the surface, they'll sprout.

The moral? Don't cultivate unless you have to. Always cover your soil with plants (vegetables, lawn, flowers, ground covers) or mulch; otherwise, nature will cover it for you with her own trusted allies—the weeds.

untrained eye. But we all make mistakes—in my first spring of gardening, I nurtured a patch of chickweed before realizing it wasn't a treasured garden flower. If you're afraid of pulling out the flowers and keeping the weeds, it's worth identifying your perennials with a label so you'll know where they are (or at least where they're supposed to be) in spring. One hint that you've pulled out a desirable plant is the bit of potting soil left around the roots if the plant was container-grown.

If you do pull a plant out by mistake, replant it, water it, provide temporary cover from the sun to aid its recovery, and chances are it will live. (I did this once, my hand automatically pulling everything in sight, including a tiny, very slow-growing tree I'd started from seed—and it survived my mistreatment.)

Another clue to what's a weed is that most weeds start growing and greening up before the perennials get going in spring. Many weeds have tiny flowers that seem to bloom and go to seed in a nanosecond—by comparison, desirable garden flowers tend to be much larger and bloom longer. Keep your eyes peeled and you'll soon learn to recognize which bits of greenery are weeds and which are your treasured plants.

Weeding between the lines

The really maddening thing about weeds is the speed with which they reproduce. Turn your back for a week and you have to wonder if it's game over for the garden. Even if you think it's too late, just get in there and start weeding. Every bit will pay off.

Fortunately, smart gardeners have figured out ways to outsmart weeds. Here's how:

- Do a thorough job of getting rid of grasses and perennial weeds before you plant. Never dig or till a weedy or grassy area and plant directly into it—you'll regret it for years. Follow the instructions in Chapter 3 for preparing the soil.
- When you see a weed, pull it—now. And go after weeds when they're small—it's easier to pull or hoe out a tiny weed than one that's grown a taproot halfway to China.
- Never let weeds go to seed and don't add weed seeds to your compost. Annual weeds can spawn a couple of generations in a single season if they're allowed to seed. After two or three seasons of

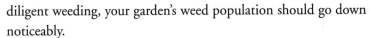

diligent weeding, your garden's weed population should go down noticeably.

- Lawns can have weeds, and the grass itself forms seeds, so don't shoot clippings into your planting beds when you're mowing.
- Prevention saves tons of work, and mulch is the best preventive there is. (Remember the mulch section in Chapter 3?) I always layer mulch over bare soil between my plants, as this prevents most weed seeds from germinating and makes any weeds that do get a start easier to pull out. Once my garden beds are established, I'm amazed at how few weeds there are. (It's the only way I know to have your cake and eat it too—big beds that are manageable.) Bottom line? Cover your soil with desirable plants and mulch, and weeds have fewer opportunities to get a toehold.

Tackling the really tough cases

Pulling, hoeing, and mulching are effective for most annual and biennial weeds. But perennial weeds can easily regenerate from small pieces of root left in the ground.

The most effective and easiest way to dispatch them is to use a glysophate-based non-selective herbicide such as Roundup. Spray the weeds carefully, following the manufacturer's directions. If you prefer not to use herbicide, there's another solution—smothering the weeds. But like many non-chemical methods, this calls for patience. Here's what to do:

- Spread a 2" (5 cm) layer of compost or well-rotted manure.
- Add a 4" (10 cm) layer of organic mulch such as straw or shredded leaves and top it with a sheet of black plastic or old carpeting.
- Leave in place for one season. One year of this treatment should do the trick, but if the roots aren't dead the following spring, leave the whole shebang in place for another season.

What a weedy lawn may be telling you

A thick, healthy lawn should crowd out most weeds. Many of the weeds that invade lawns—prostrate knotweed, dandelions, plantain, and thistles—are signs of poor soil fertility and soil compaction from heavy wear (lots of foot, bike, or wheelbarrow traffic). If you correct these conditions, your lawn will stand a better chance of out-competing weeds. (See Chapter 7 for tips on improving the health of your lawn.)

Another common lawn problem is moss, which could be caused by soil compaction, acidic soil, or too much shade. Some solutions:

- If your soil is compacted, improve it by aerating and top-dressing (adding a thin layer consisting of a mixture of compost and well-rotted manure and raking it in with a leaf rake).
- If your soil is acidic, apply horticultural lime according to the directions on the package.
- Lawn grasses don't thrive in heavy shade, so if excessive shade is the problem, consider replacing the grass with a shade-tolerant ground cover.
- If you can't beat them, join them—why not throw in the towel and have a moss garden? (As with so many things in gardening, there's even a book on this topic! See Resources on page 185.)

A Cure for What Bugs You

As you grow your garden, you're going to notice insects like never before, so it's best to get used to the idea that it's impossible (and not even desirable) to have a garden without them. If bug-free is your goal, give it up now and take up a less lively hobby—a good garden teams with life, and that's how it should be.

You may be surprised to learn that the more insects in your garden, the better. And herein lies the paradox. The key to a healthy balance between the eaters and what's getting eaten is diversity: having as many different plants—and insects—as you can. In his admirable book *Insects and Gardens*, entomologist and keen gardener Eric Grissell explains: "The goal is to build layer upon layer of simple plant diversity until the insect-plant and insect-insect interactions become so complex that they take care of themselves, and we poor simple-minded gardeners won't need to worry about such things."

Variety truly is the spice of life in the garden. I've always gardened whole hog—my beds are overflowing with an assortment of plants, from trees and shrubs to tons of perennials—and there's no bare soil if I can help it. Even my vegetables don't grow solo but share their space with flowers and herbs.

Yes, I live with some chewed leaves and the odd destroyed plant, and not everything I try works—that's gardening! However, when a problem becomes really bad—such as the shrub rose in the perennial bed that became nothing more than a magnet for Japanese beetles—I toss the plant and try something else. Rose fanciers might feel sorry for me, but rather than battle the beetles, I've chosen to have a nice garden without roses, thank you very much. I'll get my diversity from other plants.

Unfortunately, a few troublesome pests (such as my nemesis, the Japanese beetles—more on them in a minute) have given all insects a bad rap. Experts estimate that only about 1% of insects should be truly called pests. And most of the time, pest populations build up because of environmental situations that create an imbalance in insect populations. Some of the worst pests (like those Japanese beetles) are insects that have been introduced to North America and proliferated because they have few natural enemies here. Many insects don't feed on plants—at least not to the point of killing them—but in fact on each other. In addition, countless insects, such as bees, wasps, moths, and flies are important plant allies, doing the job of pollination so the plants can set seed. Other insects consume real pests and clean up dead bugs and decomposing plant materials.

Think of it this way: Most insects are just trying to make a living—like the rest of us—and, in the end, many insects become food for species we humans appreciate more, such as birds and fish.

One interesting and counterintuitive suggestion Grissell makes in his book is to stop being such a tidy gardener. The folks who vacuum up every bit of garden debris do the garden's insect residents—and their plants—a disservice. You don't have to chop down all those perennials in the fall—many perennials and grasses look just fine over winter. Old plants, plant debris, and mulch are all great overwintering spots for insects, (which is why you're usually told to clean the garden up.) Now there's evidence that keeping most of the plant foliage intact over winter is a good idea, because this environment provides cover for a diverse population of insects.

Grissell recommends cutting back the dead foliage when spring comes, then chopping up as much as you can and tucking it between the plants to literally compost in place. What a neat idea: If you leave the stuff to compost in place, you eliminate the need to drag it off to be composted and then dragging the compost back to the garden. If your garden is full of plants, as he recommends, you won't see the debris once the plants have had their spring growth spurt. (Honest. I've tried this. If you have enough plants, your garden won't look messy.)

The point of creating this mulchy environment is to help stabilize the insect populations to achieve a better balance between prey and predators. But nature's balance isn't for the softhearted, Grissell writes: "Balance is what happens when nature is in harmony with itself. By harmony, I do not mean peace—there is no peace in nature. For nature to be in harmony all factions must be in constant battle."

Now you know: This is what you're getting into when you take up the gentle pastime of gardening.

Insects catching insects

What a concept: Instead of spraying something on an unwanted bug, you can order up a dose of predator bugs to go after the insects you don't want in the garden (it's called biological control, or biocontrol for short). This idea has given rise to a host of mail-order suppliers selling beneficial insects such as ladybugs and lacewings.

But the problem you're trying solve is likely to stem from a basic imbalance in the garden, and some of the commonest, garden variety bugs in nature—the unsung ants, many beetles, even spiders (which technically aren't insects, by the way)—can work wonders to maintain balance if you create the kind of garden they find hospitable—one that's rich in a variety of plants with lots of mulchy spots for them to hide in.

Most of the time, the bugs you buy just fly off into the neighborhood anyway. So save your money and get more plants to create the paradise of diversity prescribed here.

The pest defense is a good offense

All right. You now know that diversity—in both plants and insects—is your best defense. As you might have guessed, the ordinary yard —with its swath of lawn, sprinkling of annuals, evergreen foundation shrubs, and a tree or two—doesn't cut it when it comes to diversity. So how do you invite diversity into your garden? Go crazy at the garden center? Well, yes, but there's a bit more to it than that.

- Plant a variety of species—trees, shrubs, annuals, and perennials. The problem with acres of one thing is that it's a banquet laid on for the pests, easy to find, and oh so tempting. If you grow a variety of plants, any bug problems that do arise won't affect everything in the garden.

- Grow more native plants. Plants adapted to your climate, soil, and moisture conditions are often better able to grow without problems. Now, this doesn't mean giving up your old-fashioned garden favorites—just add more native trees, shrubs, and perennials. My two favorites in this category are Joe Pye weed (*Eupatorium*) and, believe it or not, goldenrod. Native plant gardening is growing in popularity and there are many good books on the topic (see Resources on page 185).

- Diverse plant species attract birds, frogs and toads (a single toad can devour about 10,000 insects in a growing season), and helpful insects that eat thousands of other insects. To attract them, provide a source of fresh water for your garden allies. Add one or all of the following: a garden pond, a bird bath, a pot filled with water, or a large saucer at ground level. (To avoid breeding mosquitoes, add fish to your pond and be sure to change the water in pots or birdbaths regularly.)

- Entice beneficial insects into your garden by planting dill, cilantro, fennel, yarrow, and parsley and allowing them to go to flower. Plant herbs and flowers among your vegetables.

- Pests and diseases tend to leave healthy plants alone and zoom in on stressed plants. To avoid stressing plants, pay attention to the proper growing conditions. Like people, plants get stressed when their needs aren't met, such as a sun lover planted in shade, or a lover of cool summers forced to exist in a hot, humid climate.

Use safer pest controls

If you opt to spray, do it thoughtfully and only if necessary. Remember that all products ending in "cide"—the suffix means "to kill"—are meant to destroy something, so always use them with respect for yourself and the environment. If the label says to wear gloves when mixing and spraying, do it. Be sure to spray on a day that isn't windy.

A variety of less toxic pest-control products are listed below. These all break down quickly and, once broken down, they don't linger. Organic versus chemical isn't the point here (though the products listed are acceptable to most organic gardeners)—the point is minimizing your own exposure to toxicity and choosing products that break down in the environment quickly.

Follow directions, and avoid killing beneficial insects by treating only the problem spot. If you're spraying for an insect problem, remember that most modern pesticides are designed to work on contact. If you don't actually hit the problem bug with the product, you're not doing any good at all. And before you go spray-crazy, try find out what the insect is, whether it is really necessary to spray, whether the product you have chosen will do the job effectively and safely, and if you're even spraying at the right time.

A few points about what is available:

- **Lime-sulphur dormant oil spray** is a time-honored preventive organic spray used as both an insecticide and a fungicide. It is commonly applied in early spring to smother overwintering pests and to prevent fungal disease on woody plants. The time to spray is when the buds are swollen but not yet open. It is useful for many woody plants but should not sprayed be on beech (*Fagus*), butternut (*Juglans cinerea*), Colorado blue spruce (*Picea pungens*), Douglas fir (*Pseudotsuga menziesii*), hickory (*Carya*), holly (*Ilex*), sugar maple (*Acer saccharum*), Japanese maple (*Acer palmatum*), or walnut (*Juglans nigra*).
- **Insecticidal soap** destroys soft-bodied pests such as aphids, mites, and whiteflies, but the spray must hit the insects to work. For bad infestations, spray every three days over a two-week period. Some plants are injured by insecticidal soap, so check the label before using.
- **Pyrethrum dusts or sprays,** derived from the flowers of pyrethrum daisies, attack insects' central nervous systems and break down quickly in air, light, and heat. These products are effective against many flying, chewing, and sucking insects but are non-selective, which means they don't discriminate between good and bad insects and kill any they contact. They are also toxic to fish, so avoid using near ponds or streams. (Curious about whether planting pyrethrum daisies would work too? Actually, no—the products are effective because the active agent is very concentrated.)

- **Bacillus thuringiensis,** a naturally occurring bacterium, disrupts digestion in caterpillars and other leaf-eaters. Know the pest before buying this product—different strains of the bacterium are used for specific insects.

Those nasty JBs

Japanese beetles are found in many parts of North America, particularly in the eastern half of the continent. If you don't have this pest, consider yourself lucky.

They spend about 10 months of the year underground as a white grub that lies in the soil in a curled, C-shaped form. Grubs feed on the roots of plants, and especially lawn grasses, and can damage lawns if the population is heavy—about 15 grubs per square yard (square meter) is considered heavy. The winged adults, with their distinctive metallic green bodies, emerge in midsummer, usually toward the end of June and are active on warm, sunny days over a six-week to two-month period. They feed on many perennials and some trees and shrubs, but love to chow down on roses—both flowers and leaves.

NATURAL CONTROLS

Extremely dry summers interfere with their reproduction, so letting your lawn go dormant in a drought can be helpful (even more so if all the neighbors don't water their lawns either). Other insects and birds (especially starlings) feed on the grubs and, less fortunately, raccoons and skunks dig up lawns to get at them.

Because the adults fly only in the daytime, it's easy to knock them off plants and into a container of soapy water early in the morning and at dusk, but you'll have to do this regularly during the weeks the adults are active. (I have spent many an hour dispatching hundreds of JBs this way. Ah, the joys of revenge!)

Milky spore disease can infect and kill beetle grubs in the soil but is harmless to people, animals, other insects, and plants. It is available in the U.S. (but not in Canada) in a powdered form. However, it isn't very effective in cool, wet, heavy soils, and beetles can still fly into your garden from other sites. It works best if applied throughout a neighborhood.

There are Japanese beetle traps on the market, but unless everyone on your street uses them, the traps could actually attract more beetles to your yard.

GRUB KILLERS

You can apply insecticides to lawns to destroy the grubs before they become adult beetles. For best results, follow the manufacturer's instructions to the letter, particularly about the amounts to use and the timing. The grubs are easier to kill in early to midsummer, soon after they hatch.

Alternatively, you might investigate organic methods, such as parasitic nematodes—microscopic roundworms that lay their eggs on the grubs and thus kill them. They come in a powdered form that you mix with water and spray onto your lawn. The best time to do this depends on where you live, so read the directions carefully. Nematodes are best used when it's warm and moist.

PROTECTING AGAINST ADULTS ON PLANTS

Spraying with a pyrethrum-based insecticide or one that includes insecticidal soap and pyrethrum can protect the foliage and flowers of susceptible plants. Unfortunately, these products can also kill bees and many other beneficial insects. To minimize this, spray beetles on affected plants only, and do it at dawn or dusk, when honeybees and other flying insects are less active. Begin spraying as soon as the beetles appear and before they can do too much damage. Use insecticides only on plants for which they are indicated.

Remedies for Sick Plants

Plants aren't sitting ducks. In fact, they have an amazing ability to resist diseases if they're healthy to begin with. Here are some useful tips for boosting your garden's immune system:

- To avoid fungal diseases, water deeply early in the day, then let the top layer of soil dry out before watering again. Wet leaves overnight can invite fungal problems. Many diseases thrive in constant moisture and poor air circulation, and an excessively wet growing season can bring problems.
- If fungal diseases such as black spot on roses appear, clean up affected leaves and throw them into the garbage, not the compost bin.

> ## Making your own fungicide spray
>
> Dissolve 1 to 2 teaspoons of baking soda with a few drops of dish soap in half a gallon (2 liters) of water. Use this spray as a preventive measure on plants that are susceptible to fungal problems, because once a fungus appears, it's difficult to remedy except by cutting off and disposing of affected leaves.

- Some plants are especially susceptible to certain diseases. For example, the list of diseases that affect crabapple trees is awe-inspiring—apple scab, rust, fire blight, leaf spot, and powdery mildew. Fortunately, disease-resistant varieties are available; look for them by checking plant tags or doing some research in books or on the Web. (After all, you do this sort of scouting around before buying a fridge. Why not be equally careful when buying a tree?)
- Lilacs, phlox, and bee balm (*Monarda*) regularly get mildew on their leaves. This doesn't harm the plant, only its late-summer appearance, but to avoid the problem, look for mildew-resistant varieties.

Oh Deer, Oh Deer

Some people love having Bambi visit their yards, but in recent years, deer have become a problem for gardeners and homeowners. The deer population is increasing, even in urban areas, partly because development has encroached on their habitat, they have fewer predators, and, in some localities, laws that protect wildlife have been put into place. Attractive as they are, gardeners would appreciate them more if they weren't so partial to devouring favorite perennials and shrubs.

Deer are most active just after dark and before dawn—times when you're unlikely to be around to scare them off—but short of taking up hunting, gardeners can still try a number of methods to keep deer out of their yards.

The most effective, but also the most expensive and work-intensive option, is deer fencing. The fence should be at least 5' to 8' (1.5 m to 2.4 m) high. Sloping your fence at an angle so the top points away from your garden increases its effectiveness. Other measures include:

- **Netting:** If you have just a few plants to protect, you can wrap plastic netting around them or put it on the ground around the plant—deer hate stepping on netting.
- **Repellents:** Garden suppliers and home centers carry a number of products to spray on plants to make them taste or smell bad. Some types of soap, particularly strong-smelling ones, can be effective, at least until deer get used to them. Cut bars in half or in quarters and hang them in cloth bags to keep them from dissolving too fast. Suspend bags about every 10' (3 m) or so on woody plants, fence posts, or stakes and replenish as needed.
- **Hair:** Some folks swear by human hair from salons. Again, put it in cloth bags around the garden so deer can readily catch the scent. Dog hair from a dog-grooming establishment might also do the trick.
- **The urine of predators:** This stuff, courtesy of wolves and coyotes, can make deer nervous enough to steer clear of your place. You have to wonder how it's collected, but it's available from garden suppliers and over the Internet.
- **Noisemakers:** This includes radios or ultrasonic devices. Ultrasonic repellent devices are expensive and often not as effective as

Deer-resistant plants

Perennials	Deciduous trees	Evergreen trees	Evergreen shrubs	Deciduous shrubs
Brown-eyed Susan (*Rudbeckia*)	Bradford or Chanticleer pear (*Pyrus* calleryana 'Bradford', 'Chanticleer')	Douglas fir (*Pseudotsuga menziesii*)	Bird's nest spruce (*Picea abies* 'Nidiformis')	Anthony Waterer Spirea (*Spiraea* x *bumalda* 'Anthony Waterer')
Coral bells (*Heuchera*)		Scotch pine (*Pinus sylvestris*)	Dwarf Alberta spruce (*Picea glauca* var. albertiana)	
Coreopsis	Red maple (*Acer rubrum*)	Spruce, most types (*Picea* species)		Bayberry (*Myrica pensylvanica*)
Cornflower (*Centaurea*)	Heritage or river birch (*Betula nigra* 'Heritage')		Dwarf blue spruce (*Picea pungens* 'R. H. Montgomery')	Burning bush (*Euonymus alatus* 'Compactus')
Evening primrose (*Oenothera*)				
Lenten rose (*Helleborus*)	Paper birch (*Betula papyrifera*)		Japanese garden juniper (*Juniperis procumbens* 'Nana')	Cinquefoil (*Potentilla fruticosa*)
Ornamental grasses	Serviceberry (*Amelanchier canadensis*)		Lily-of-the-valley shrub (*Pieris japonica*)	Cotoneaster (*Cotoneaster horizontalis*, *Cotoneaster dammeri*)
Ornamental onions (*Allium* species)	White, pin, and scarlet oak (*Quercus* species)			
Perennial sage (*Salvia*)			Mugo pine (*Pinus mugo*)	
Purple coneflower (*Echinacea*)				
Russian sage (*Perovskia*)				
Shasta daisy (*Leucanthemum*)				
Speedwell (*Veronica*)				
Yarrow (*Achillea*)				

billed. Unfortunately, deer soon become accustomed to familiar sounds and objects, so these methods are successful only if you move the ultrasonic transmitter or the radio quite frequently. If you use a radio, it doesn't have to be very loud, but it's best to tune to an all-night talk show, as human voices are scarier for deer than music. (Obviously, noisemakers are not an option if the sounds are loud enough to disturb neighbors.)

Plants deer don't like

Deer will eat almost anything if they're ravenous enough, but they'll usually steer clear of some plants. Normally, they avoid anything with a strong taste or smell, and they don't like chewing hairy leaves, but remember if they're hungry enough, deer may try plants they normally avoid. See the chart on page 157 for a sampler of deer-resistant plants.

Other Critters

Rabbits, mice, and voles (mouse-like creatures) can nibble the bark off young trees and shrubs, especially in winter, so protect them with either plastic guards that you wrap around young trucks or a wire mesh guard you can cut out of hardware cloth. Because this stuff doesn't look super fantastic, be sure to remove it in spring.

Chapter 14

To Everything There is a Season: What to Do When

If it's Tuesday, the first week of March, do this.

Well, not exactly. This chapter will clue you in on what to do when, but guidelines are given in seasonal terms—early and mid spring, summer, fall, and winter—instead of month by month. When appropriate, you'll be directed to the chapter in which the how-to is explained in more detail. But don't panic. *You won't have to do every last thing on this list.* Besides, it's unlikely you'll be growing all the different types of plants mentioned.

In fact, the best way to use this chapter is not to read it through in one go—that's guaranteed to be overwhelming and a tad repetitive—but to consult it at the beginning of each season to find out what you should be aware of and what jobs are best done at that time of year. Gardening is seasonally adjusted, you know!

And don't worry. You'll get the hang of gardening by sticking with it for a season or two. Basically, plants are programmed to grow, and as long as you don't do anything too bizarre, they will oblige you—

except perhaps for the odd one that's just ornery. If you don't do everything I've listed here, your garden won't fail. (If you don't do anything at all, it probably will—but you knew that already.)

With certain jobs, timing is vital: transplanting and pruning, for example. Leaving either of those tasks too late can create problems. If you prune a lilac too late in the season, for instance, you will cut off the buds that produce next year's flowers. And you don't want to move shrubs or perennials in the heat of midsummer—the stress can kill them. Once you've been gardening for a few years, you'll be a lot more in tune with the seasons than you ever thought possible—that's actually one of the chief joys of gardening. So here goes your seasonal guide.

Early Spring

This is an exciting time and perhaps the busiest of the gardening year (fall is the second busiest). Migrating birds are returning, and the buds on trees and shrubs are swelling but not out yet. Around the neighborhood early bulbs such as snowdrops and crocuses are in bloom. Everybody's got spring fever.

To do: Around the yard

- Start winter cleanup when the lawn is no longer sopping wet and planting beds stop being a sea of mud.
- Remove tree guard or burlap winter protection from any trees or shrubs. Plastic tree guards shouldn't be left in place over the summer; they don't exactly look great and they don't allow air movement around the base of the trunk.
- Transplant existing shrubs you want to move before they begin to leaf out. (See page 119.)
- Weeds start growing vigorously early, so when you spot them, go to it. Getting on top of the weeding now means a lot less work later. They are easier to remove while their roots are still shallow. (For more on weeding, see pages 144–48.)
- Apply dormant oil spray to fruit trees and woody plants to control overwintering insects. Use when the buds are swelling but the leaves haven't opened yet. (See page 152.)
- Get the lawn mower checked and sharpened, and buy fresh gas so it's ready to go.

To do: In the flower garden

- Don't be in a rush to remove winter mulch or to cut back ever-green plants such as lavender until temperatures are reliably warm.
- Start cutting back any dead perennial foliage from last season (trimmings can go into the compost). Cut back ornamental grasses. (See page 87.)
- Remove winter protection of mounded earth from roses; prune rose bushes before they start to leaf out.
- Once the soil has dried out—if you pick up a handful, it should fall apart, not stick together like glue—start to dig beds and add compost or manure in preparation for planting. (See pages 26–33.)
- Edge flower beds to keep grass in bounds.

Lawn   Planting Bed

For an edge that prevents lawn from creeping into flower beds, make a vertical cut with a spade as deep as the grass roots go. The bed edge should taper gradually. Recut the lawn edge two or more times through the season to keep it sharp.

To do: In the vegetable garden

- If you're adventurous and can provide artificial light or a sunny windowsill, start seeds indoors of warm-season vegetables such as tomatoes and peppers.
- Plant early crops—radishes, lettuce, and spinach—outdoors. (See pages 126–27.)

Mid *to* Late Spring

Tulips, daffodils, and lilacs are in full bloom. The grass is growing so vigorously you need to cut it almost twice a week. Frost is almost a distant memory, though in northerly regions it can still sneak up on you.

To do: Around the yard

- Plant new trees and shrubs. (See pages 111–12.)
- Prune broad-leaved evergreen plants and evergreen or deciduous hedges. Prune spring-flowering shrubs right after their blossoms fade. (See pages 113–19.)
- To encourage thick, compact growth on pines and other needled evergreens, pinch the new candles (a hort term for the new growth on evergreens) to remove half of the new growth.
- Repair dead spots in lawn with seed; fill holes with compost or soil to level uneven spots and reseed. (See pages 65–66.)
- Start mowing the lawn. (See pages 59–60.)
- Water newly planted trees and shrubs, ground cover plants and perennials if there isn't enough rain. (See Chapter 4.)
- Keep weeding. Weeds are growing most vigorously now. Getting on top of it now will mean less weeding later on in the season and weeds won't get a chance to go to seed.
- Plant container gardens. (See Chapter 12.)
- Aerate lawn. (See sidebar on page 60.)

When to prune shrubs

Type of shrub	Best time to prune
Spring-flowering shrubs: forsythia, lilac, purple sand cherry, flowering almond, mock orange	Right after flowering
Summer- or fall-flowering shrubs: hydrangea, rose of Sharon, spirea, buddleia	Early spring
Azaleas and rhododendrons	Right after flowering
Formal hedges	Late spring or early summer and again in fall (if needed)
Evergreen and broadleaf evergreen shrubs	In early spring, just as new buds begin to open

To do: In the flower garden

- Continue to plant and transplant perennials. (See pages 84–85.)
- Divide perennials and ornamental grasses that need it. (See pages 87–90.)
- Plant frost-tender annuals and dahlias and summer-flowering bulbs such as gladioli after the last frost date for your region. (See pages 84–85.)
- Label any new plants so you'll remember what they are or draw a map of your garden.
- Make note of any gaps that could be filled with spring bulbs for next year and add new plants to fill gaping holes now.
- Mulch your flower beds. (See pages 34–36.)
- Stake perennials such as delphiniums and peonies before they've grown too tall (bamboo sticks and string do a better job than most commercial contraptions).
- Water if it's dry.
- Apply fertilizer if needed.

To do: In the vegetable garden

- Plant warm-season vegetables such as tomatoes and herbs after the last frost date for your region. (See pages 125, 129–30 and 132–35.)
- Mulch around vegetables with straw. (See page 35.)

Early Summer

All your early attention is paying off and plants are growing vigorously. Early-summer flowers such as peonies and irises are in bloom.

To do: Around the yard

- Shear deciduous or evergreen hedges.
- Mow the lawn as often as needed, but don't remove more than one third of the grass blades at a one time. (See pages 59–60.)
- Keep weeding.
- Keep watering as needed, especially newly planted trees, shrubs, and perennials.
- Keep an eye out for insect and disease problems. (See Chapter 13.)

- Deadhead rhododendrons and lilacs and prune any spring-flowering shrubs that need it. (See pages 118–19.)

To do: In the flower garden

- Deadhead annuals, roses, and perennials to groom the garden and encourage repeat blooming. (See pages 86–87.)
- Begin to spray roses every week with a fungicide or baking soda solution to protect against black spot disease. (See pages 151–52 and 154–55.)
- Pinch asters and mums to encourage compact growth and more blooms. (See sidebar on page 87.)
- Cut down yellowing bulb foliage. (See page 86.)

To do: In the vegetable garden

- Keep weeding and watering where necessary.
- Begin harvesting and eating or preserving cool-season veggies. (See pages 127 and 128–29.)

Midsummer

The lazy hazy days of summer mean that you can relax a bit more. The spring planting jobs are done and hot, dry weather often slows down plant growth. Walk around the garden with a drink in hand and admire your handiwork.

To do: Around the yard

- Keep watering the plants to help them through the heat and dryness; if you're going on holidays, arrange to have someone water the garden and your container plants.
- Raise the mower setting to cut the lawn higher so it can better withstand hot, dry weather. (See pages 59–60.)
- To save water, consider allowing your lawn to go dormant; it will green up again when the rains return. (See page 61.)
- Remove weeds before they set seed; look under plants for stray weeds you've missed.

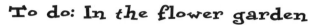

To do: In the flower garden

- Keep deadheading perennials to encourage a second flush of bloom. (See page 87.)
- Pinch back asters and chrysanthemums one last time. (See sidebar on page 87.)
- Cut back any rampant growth or overly exuberant plants that are smothering their neighbors and prune back perennials that go dormant (bleeding heart and poppies).
- Take garden notes and/or photographs to plan future plantings. For more ideas, go to the garden center and see what they're selling that's in bloom now.
- If the color in your garden seems to be over, make a list of plants to add to give flower and foliage color in late summer and fall. (See page 83 for a list of bloom times of favorite perennials.)

To do: In the vegetable garden

- Check vegetables and start harvesting as they ripen. (See pages 128–29.)
- Continue to weed and water and check for pest or disease problems as necessary.

Early Fall

The season begins to wind down, the air is cooler and seems fresher, daylight grows shorter, and early trees start to turn color. Late-blooming perennials such as sedums, asters, mums, and ornamental grasses are in flower; the first frosts are just around the corner.

To do: In the yard

- Once they're past their prime, empty containers of annuals and store frost-sensitive containers in the basement or the garage.
- Continue to water if it's dry.
- Aerate the lawn and reseed any dead or thin spots. (See sidebar on page 60 and pages 65–66.)
- This is a great time to lay sod or start a lawn from seed. (See pages 64–66.)
- Prepare soil for any new beds you want to have ready for spring planting. (See page 29.)

- This is a good time to plan or do landscaping projects, such as walls, walkways, patios, and decks. (See Chapter 15.)

To do: In the flower garden

- Don't be in a great rush to cut back all your perennials—foliage that's coloring up and seed heads can be beautiful, and the seeds provide food for migrating birds. Just cut back plants that are diseased, those looking past their prime, or those that may become "weeds" if they're allowed to self-seed too freely. (See page 87.)
- If you have too little color in the garden now, visit the garden center for some ideas on late-season flowers to add, and take advantage of seasonal sales.
- Plant or transplant perennials. Divide overgrown perennials—this is the time to divide and move peonies and bearded and Siberian irises. (See pages 87–90.)
- Remove summer annuals that are past their prime and plant mums and colorful kale for fall interest.
- Make notes about garden changes or plants that you might want to move in the spring.
- Buy spring-flowering bulbs while they're in plentiful supply.

To do: In the vegetable garden

- After harvesting, remove spent plant material in the vegetable garden and add to the compost.

Mid to Late Fall

The first frosts have arrived and in colder regions snow is on its way. Daylight-saving time ends and, rats, it's getting dark earlier all the time. Leaves are coloring and dropping. Time to get the garden ready for winter.

To do: Around the yard

- If you spray for lawn weeds, this is about the most effective time to do it. (See page 147.)
- Continue to water trees, especially evergreens, until the ground freezes. Evergreens need a good store of moisture going into winter

because they don't lose their leaves, which means they continue to transpire (give off water vapor) through the cold months.

- Complete the removal of fallen leaves from the lawn.
- Move shrubs or small trees that you have earmarked for relocation.
- Consider shredding fall leaves and using them as winter mulch. Add some shredded leaves to the compost pile. (See page 32–34.)
- Do one last weeding and discard any weeds that have seeds on them in the garbage instead of the compost.
- In many regions, this is a good time to plant trees and shrubs. (See pages 109–10 and 111–12.)
- Put plastic or wire mesh (hardware cloth) tree guards around the slender trunks of any new trees and shrubs to protect them from gnawers such as rabbits and mice, and make sure the tree guards go high enough, over the snow line.
- Do a final grass cutting and empty the mower of gas. Consider getting it serviced and the blade sharpened now so it's ready for spring.
- Apply late lawn fertilizer. (See pages 62–63.)

To do: In the flower garden

- To cut back or not to cut back: That is the decision. Whether you prune off all dying perennial foliage in fall is up to you. Some

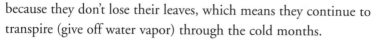

Don't go crazy with burlap covers on evergreen trees and shrubs. It's extra work and they are ugly. The whole point of evergreens is to give you something green to look at in the winter, and contrary to popular belief, most hardy evergreens *do not need* burlap wraps for winter protection. If the plants are exposed to salt spray from the road, burlap may help, but it should be a double layer, not a single layer. To avoid having to cover your evergreens, don't plant them near a roadway that gets salted.

If you feel you must protect certain broadleaf evergreens, such as rhododendrons, from exposure to winter sun and wind, hammer stakes or bamboo poles into the ground around the shrub and surround it with burlap. Or use an anti-desiccant spray that coats foliage with a protective waxy film. Better still, choose tougher plants that don't need to be coddled over the winter.

gardeners like to leave seed heads and dried foliage for winter inter-est and to feed birds; others prefer to leave neat beds ready for a show of spring-flowering bulbs. A good compromise is to remove leaves and stalks that frost turns to mush and any that are diseased, but keep ornamental grasses and the perennials with seedheads that provide winter food to birds. If you want to cut them back, prune perennials to 4" or 5" (10 to 13 cm) off the ground.

- Pull out any last frosted annuals and add spent plant material to your compost (diseased leaves should go into the garbage, not the compost).
- Do a final weeding and edging of flower beds.
- Plant bulbs. (See pages 85–86.)
- Dig up and store tender bulbs such as cannas, dahlias, and gladioli after the first hard frost that blackens their leaves, wash off any soil that's still clinging, and leave them exposed to air in a basket indoors for a couple of weeks. When they're dry, store in vermiculite or dry peat (available at garden centers) in paper bags or cardboard boxes. Overwinter in a cool, frost-free place.
- Hill up hybrid tea roses with soil for winter protection if necessary. (See box below for details.)
- Spread finished compost on garden beds between plants.

Getting roses through the winter

Many roses—hybrid teas, floribundas, and grandiflo-ras—need winter protection in colder regions. (Many hardy shrub roses do not.) Here's what to do:

- Remove fallen rose leaves from around each plant to help prevent a recurrence of such common problems as black spot.
- Don't prune roses back now—wait for early spring. The excep-tion is rose bushes taller than 6' (1.8 m), which can be cut to a more manageable height of about 3' (1 m) tall.
- Once the ground starts to freeze, hill or mound up soil 6" to 8" (15 to 20 cm) high around the base of each plant. A rose collar, available in most garden centers, can be used to help keep soil in place. Don't use soil from around plants for hilling—bring in additional soil.

Downing tools for the season

Imagine finding all your garden tools in good working order come spring. Heck, sometimes I have trouble just *finding* them again. Here's what you can do now to help then:

- Remove soil from hand tools. Sharpen spades, hoes, pruners, loppers, and pruning saws. Tighten loose screws or nuts; lubricate moving parts and springs. Repair any broken handles.
- To prevent rust, spray exposed metal parts and cutting edges with a penetrating oil such as WD-40.
- Wash and rinse sprayers used for insect, disease, or weed control, following manufacturer's directions. Store upside down.
- Drain all water from hoses. Store them kink-free in a dry place on a hose reel or loosely coiled rather than hanging on a hook or nail. Drain hose bibs at the house.
- Power equipment—lawn mowers, tillers, and chippers—should be cleaned of grease, dirt, and plant material. If DIY isn't your style, take your mower in for maintenance now—it's a slow time at the repair shops, so you'll beat the lineups in spring.
- Two-cycle engines that run on a gas and oil mixture should have it removed. To do this, run the engine with the choke open until the fuel runs out. Don't store gasoline—it deteriorates quickly—and never use old gasoline in your equipment.

- Once the ground freezes, apply a layer of winter mulch to perennial beds—don't do this too early or you'll provide winter housing for rodents. (See sidebar on page 35 and page 36.)

To do: In the vegetable garden

- Remove any remaining debris such as frosted annuals and spent vegetable plants.
- Spread finished compost or well-rotted manure over the veggie garden. (See page 31.)
- Protect bare soil in the vegetable or annual garden with a mulch of straw or leaves.

Winter

Though many gardeners dislike winter, I actually love it. It's time to take a break, put your feet up, comb through all the new seed catalogues, and dream of next summer's absolutely fabulous garden.

To do: Around the yard

- Prune away storm-damaged branches promptly. This prevents tearing the bark.
- Nudge snow loads off your trees and shrubs gently—stems can be quite brittle in winter.
- Avoid using salt to melt snow and ice, as it is toxic to most plants. Instead, use environmentally friendly ice melters or sawdust, sand, or cat litter.
- Check on dahlia, canna, and gladiolus bulbs in your basement occasionally for rotting and/or drying out. Discard any dubious bulbs and sprinkle a tiny bit of water over them if they appear to be drying out.

- Prune deciduous trees and shrubs in late winter. (See pages 116–19.)
- Read gardening books, and look at catalogues and order seeds and plants for next season.

Help!

My bulbs think it's spring

Have you ever noticed spring-flowering bulbs coming up too soon, in late fall and even midwinter? Don't panic. This is quite common with newly planted bulbs, especially in a winter that's milder than normal. (Bulbs that have been in the ground for a while seem to know better than to start growing prematurely.)

A thick blanket of snow gives the best protection from the cold and from drying winter winds, but if you normally don't get much snow or the winter is mild, chop the branches off your used Christmas tree (if you need more, grab the ones your neighbors have put out for pickup) and place the boughs over bulb foliage. Remove them in early spring when the weather warms up and the bulbs are ready for their spring fling.

Chapter 15

Mission Possible: From Ho-hum Yard to Glorious Garden

Most garden books for beginners tell you to start with a plan. Getting it on paper will help you avoid big mistakes, they insist. The trouble is, you're clueless about gardening. When you can't tell a hosta from a daylily, much less what trees and shrubs will grow well for you, how can you possibly make a plan?

Most expert gardeners got that way by getting their hands dirty. Rather than following a plant-by-number pattern, a surprising number of stunning gardens have taken shape bit by bit over many seasons—without a grand plan. Good gardeners aren't afraid to move plants or even beds around until the garden feels right. So don't be anxious about trial and error—the fact is that most gardens evolve.

That's why I left the topic of designing and planning your garden to the end. Now that you've had a chance to learn the horticultural ropes, you should have a few good ideas about what you'd like to do in your own garden—and that means you're now in a much better position to consider an overall scheme for it.

Survey Says

When you buy a house, a copy of a survey map showing the location of buildings and property lines usually comes with the deed. Have a good look at it. You don't want to plant or build something that could be on your neighbor's property—you might be forced to undo it.

Before you start digging, find out where underground service lines run for hydro, gas, water, and telephone lines. Keep lines above ground in mind too, especially when you're planting trees. On many rural properties, you'll have to locate the septic tank and leaching field, as this is an area you need to keep free of trees (it's also one that you shouldn't drive vehicles over).

The survey is also a good way to start getting ideas on paper. Trace it out, then get the measuring tape and mark in other features, such as existing trees and shrubs (only the ones that are keepers). Buy see-through tracing paper and try out different ideas for planting beds, patios, and walkways before you put a spade in the ground.

It Takes More Than Plants

While plants are central to gardens, it takes more than flora and foliage to make an appealing garden—and by "garden" I mean the outdoor space surrounding the house, not just the planting beds. To get your place looking "gardeny," think beyond plants and look at other landscape attractions, such as patios, decks, water features, trellises, and paths. You're exterior decorating—furnishing your outdoor space. But don't skimp on the basics—soil improvement and drainage—in a rush to get to the fun stuff.

Organize your front and back yards with both good looks and practicality in mind. In the back, you're probably going to want privacy, as well as lush plants, some shade, and a place to relax or entertain friends. At the front, you need to set off the house attractively and get visitors to the door without having to run a gauntlet of prickly shrubs.

When it comes to front yards, there's a fresh change to the North American habit of lining lumpy shrubs up against the foundation and surrounding them with lawn. Why not use creatively planted beds to

Did You Know?

A survey done by *Money* magazine shows that every dollar you spend on landscaping can provide a recovery value of 100% to 200%. That means you should be able to get back the money you spend on your landscaping project when you sell your home—and you could actually profit by up to twice what you spend.

Money doesn't really grow on trees, but the reason landscaping provides a good return on your investment is this: Given time, today's $50 tree quickly grows into tomorrow's $250 tree. And just as a well-designed landscape contributes to the "curb appeal" of your home and gets buyers inside, a poorly maintained one can them put off big-time.

bring life, texture, and color to the front of the house? While you're at it, set your plants away from that narrow strip of dry soil hugging the foundation and put them where you can actually see them from the front steps or inside the house. There, isn't that better?

Getting to Know Your Garden Patch

Like real estate, the key to garden success is location, location, location. Climate and geography will determine what plants will be happy in your garden. A big flower garden or swaths of ornamental grasses will suit larger, sunny gardens, but elegant boxwood shrubs and leafy shade lovers such as hostas and ferns go beautifully around a shady urban courtyard.

One challenging location is the spanking new neighborhood. Clean, bright, and roomy, the house is the easy part, but the landscape is featureless. Everything that might have given it character—rolling contours and existing trees—has been bulldozed away by the builder.

The big difference you should make as soon as you can is to plant trees and shrubs. Woody plants grow faster than you think, and even if you're planning to move in a few years, one or two well-chosen trees, plus some attractive shrubs, will add tons of appeal to your property. (One study demonstrated that a home with trees sells for

---

Need more ideas?

Snoop around. You can learn a lot by poking around in the neighborhood—most avid gardeners are friendly and are often willing to share their knowledge when you compliment them on their gardens. Go on garden tours and visit public gardens. Read garden books and magazines, and start a clipping file of favorite structures, plants, and plant combinations. Is there a common thread that gets your creative juices flowing?

That said, keep things simple. I've visited hodgepodge gardens that had every trendy plant and accessory going, all the elements crying for attention. And then there are the plantaholics who get so obsessed with flora and foliage that they forget to leave space in their gardens for people. (Or do they actually prefer plants to people?)

7% to 14% more than one without trees.) If you have space, plant at least one shade tree that's going to grow reasonably big. Make sure it has enough room above and below the ground, so it doesn't have to compete with underground utilities and overhead wires. Never plant a woody plant without considering its eventual height and spread.

To help you make garden decisions, consider the following:

- **How do you live?** Are you interested in sprucing up your property or do you really want to get into gardening? How much maintenance can you realistically handle?

- **What's there already?** Just because it's there doesn't mean you have to keep it. After all, you didn't promise to live with those shrubs for better or worse, till death do you part. Can they be pruned, moved, or incorporated into your new landscape or should they be cut down? (Be careful about street trees—they may not even be on your property, and many municipalities have rules about what you can and can't cut down.)

- **Are you starting from scratch?** Consider your needs and wants—an inviting space for entertaining, a privacy screen, a bed for growing a few veggies or kitchen herbs, a flower border, a kids' play area, a garden shed. Do you have enough room? If not, combine features. There's no law against growing herbs and tomatoes among flowers. A playhouse can be a fun addition to the garden shed, and once the kids outgrow it, you've got more storage.

- **How can you establish structure?** By structure, garden mavens mean the key elements—the lines of beds or patios, terraces, outbuildings, trees, or fences. A wooden arbor draped with vines can serve as the entrance from your patio to the flower garden. A gazebo could be a focal point and a destination in a larger garden. A hedge, path, or fence will create the outlines of a garden room. Garden designers call this stuff the bones of the garden.

- **How will you move through the garden?** You want to create an easy and logical movement of people, pets, vehicles, and wheelbarrows from the house to areas like the garage, garden shed, or compost pile. Make paths wide enough for two people to walk side by side, at least 4' or 5' (1.2 to 1.5 m) wide.

- **What about budget and time frame?** Sorry to bring this one up, but let's face it: Most of us never have enough money for everything we want to do in the garden (or anywhere else, for that

> ## Blinded by color?
>
> A lot of folks see gardening mainly as a way of getting color into their yards, but if you focus on flowers first, it's a bit like arranging lamps, accessories, and pictures before the walls are finished. Renowned garden design guru John Brookes advises planning and planting in the following order: first, "specials"—trees that serve as focal points—next the "skeletons," such as evergreens for year-round structure, then "decoratives"—flowering shrubs or tall grasses. Finally, you get to the "pretties"—spring- and summer-blooming perennials and fillers such as bulbs, annuals, or biennials. According to Brookes, most gardens lack structure because they start out with the "pretties."
>
> And here's another good bit of advice: Make your plant list, and then cut it in half and double the quantities of the rest.

matter). A tight budget can be overcome by reusing materials, such as old patio pavers, and by doing it yourself. It also helps to make a multi-season plan: Begin with an overall scheme and install various components over time, spreading the cost and making each do-it-yourself project more manageable—say, the fence this year, a patio the next, and a vine-covered arbor in the third season. If you're hiring a landscape contractor, ask about phasing in the landscape work over a couple of seasons.

Hiring a Landscape Pro

I like to do my own garden designs, but after we renovated our house and I struck out after several attempts on a plan for new front entry steps and a walkway, I hired a landscape architect (who was also a friend). She came up with an idea we loved but I'd never have dreamed of—I couldn't help but see the project in a certain way and from within my budget limit.

Designers widen your horizons, and because they solve problems similar to yours every day, no wonder they're better at it than you are. You may end up spending a little more (or a lot more!), but if the designer is good, you'll get the project right the first time.

Can't afford to spend a lot? A good approach is to hire people to do jobs that take more muscle or design skill than you have while you handle more manageable tasks such as preparing beds and planting shrubs and perennials. Landscapers are great for building the bones of the garden and planting bigger trees, but most of them aren't experienced with flower gardens—those are for you to play with. Landscapers tend to stick in run-of-the-garden-center plants; your choices can be more adventurous.

A few pointers on getting what you need:

- **Find good help.** Anybody with a shovel, a mower, and a pickup truck can call himself or herself a landscaper. To find good contractors, ask people with landscapes that you have admired or contact your regional professional landscapers' association. Ask to see a portfolio, references, credentials, guarantees on workmanship, and proof of insurance.

- **Stuck for ideas?** Designing a garden is daunting, especially if you've never planted anything in your life. Designers can help with the green-thumb aspects—choosing plants that suit your property—but, even more important, they'll organize outdoor spaces to enhance good features and minimize bad ones. A landscape or garden designer has knowledge and training in plants and landscape construction and can provide you with drawings, construction details, and lists of suppliers and plants. Landscape architects generally do higher-end residential or larger commercial projects; they have a degree and belong to a licensed professional association. Whomever you consult, check credentials and references and ask to see a portfolio.

- **You say formal, I say casual.** Establishing good communication is easier said than done—another good reason to have pictures on hand. If you want a French-style garden, your designer might draw up a plan that's as formal as Versailles—which won't gibe if your vision comes from a Monet painting of water lilies, tumbling lavender, and blowsy perennials.

- **Too good to be true?** Many garden centers and contractors offer "free" design services. The trouble is they may be more interested in selling their plant inventory than creating a design that meets your needs. Nothing is really free: Design costs are built into the markup on plants and materials.

- **Think ahead—way ahead.** Come spring, landscape madness grips every neighborhood in the land. Ah, the perfect time to do that long-delayed project, everybody thinks—all at the same time. Spring fever means that landscape contractors and designers are run off their feet. If you want your work done early in the season, contact the pros in the previous fall or early winter. They'll love you for it—and you'll have their full attention. By the way, fall can be a much less hectic time, and in many regions, it's still warm enough for landscape construction and planting.

Gardening Terms: Hort-Speak Demystified

Acid soil: Soil that's on acid, with a pH lower than 7.0 (and you thought high school chemistry would never come back to haunt you).

Aerate: Poking holes in the soil to increase the penetration of water and air.

Alkaline soil: Soil that isn't on acid.

Annuals: Colorful plants that live fast and die young (within one growing season).

Bare root: Dirt-cheap plants that have had the soil removed from their roots for shipping.

Biennials: For patient gardeners—plants that live for two years, normally producing flowers and seed in the second.

Bolting: What you should be doing if you accidentally get weed killer on your neighbor's prized rose bushes. Or a term used to describe vegetables that would rather have flowers than produce fruit. Often caused by late planting and warm temperatures.

Botanical name: A plant's Latin, or "scientific," name—very impressive to those who are slightly more clueless.

Bud: A favorite cold drink after an especially intense gardening session. Or the early stages of development of a flower or leaf.

Bulb: The thickened underground storage organ of plants such as daffodils and tulips. Food stored by the bulb keeps them full in their underground winter hideaways.

Chlorophyll: What makes a gardener's thumb green—the green pigment in leaves.

Compost: The higher calling your vegetable peelings, apple cores, grass clippings, and leaves achieve after rotting.

Conifer: A cone-bearing tree, usually with needle-like leaves that as an added bonus don't need to be raked. A plant used to store colored lights in mid winter.

Deadheading: Has nothing to do with an ancient rock group from the past millennium. The process of pinching off used or spent blooms to keep plants well groomed.

Dethatching: Giving your lawn a good brushing and in the process removing dead stems that build up under grass plants.

Dividing: A way to get free plants, especially perennials (a.k.a. giving them a cheap facelift).

Dormancy: The pause that refreshes, generally winter, when the garden sleeps and the gardener can afford to catch some extra winks on the weekends.

Drip line: What you're under when you share an umbrella. The area under a tree where the canopy, which acts like an umbrella, ends.

Erosion: The wearing away, washing away, or removal of soil by wind, water, and overzealous toddlers and puppies.

Evaporation: The process by which water returns to the air, which is speeded up in hot weather—too bad weeds don't evaporate.

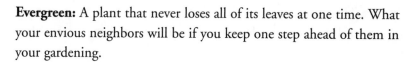

Evergreen: A plant that never loses all of its leaves at one time. What your envious neighbors will be if you keep one step ahead of them in your gardening.

Eye: An undeveloped bud that will ultimately produce new growth. Ideally, you need a good one to develop a well-landscaped garden.

Fertilizer: Stuff you can give plants to help them grow better. Usually contains nitrogen, phosphorus, and potassium.

Flat: A shallow tray for seedlings. How your peonies look after a thunderstorm if you don't stake them.

Forcing: The process of speeding a plant's growth to bloom or maturity. You may also have to do this to your kids and your spouse if you expect any help in the garden.

Frost: The freezing of moisture in the air and the soil. Tender plants will suffer extensive damage or die when exposed to frost. Best of all, after a few frosts in fall, even the gardener can lie dormant for a few months.

Germination: The sprouting of seeds, giving you tons of baby plants to play with.

Ground cover: Plants used to cover bare soil—great for gardeners who, like Mother Nature, don't like exposing their dirt.

Growing season: The number of days between the last killing frost in spring and the first killing frost in fall. Your enthusiasm for gardening should coincide with this part of the year.

Hardening off: What happens to your hands when you don't wear garden gloves. The process of getting greenhouse and indoor plants used to the real world outside.

Hardiness: The ability of a plant (or gardener) to withstand low temperatures or frost without artificial protection.

Herbaceous: A plant with soft rather than woody tissues.

Honeydew: The sticky secretion produced by sucking insects such as aphids. The to-do list for your partner to ensure he/she doesn't become a couch potato.

Humus: The stuff that really turns gardeners on—the organic part of the soil resulting from the decay of leaves and other plant or animal matter.

Hybrid: Two of a kind making one of a kind—the vigorous offspring of two related plants.

Indeterminate: A plant that continues to grow while flowering and fruiting, such as indeterminate tomatoes, which produce until frost kills them. You, when you're standing in the garden with two new plants and no idea where to put them.

Leaching: The action of water washing plant nutrients from the soil. Borrowing your neighbor's wheelbarrow again.

Leaf mold: Gardener's gold. Composted leaf litter, used as humus—a good reason not to send your leaves to the curb with the garbage.

Loam: The perfect soil few gardeners seem to have—rich soil composed of roughly equal parts of clay, sand, and silt, with at least 5% organic matter.

Manure: Organic matter, excreted by animals, used as a soil amendment and fertilizer. Has many colorful synonyms you don't want to say out loud at a garden party.

Microclimate: Variations of the climate in a local area. Usually influenced by hills or hollows or proximity to a body of water. When it's raining at your house and the sun is shining down the street.

Mulch: A blanket of loose material, such as wood chips or straw, layered over soil to control weeds and erosion and to conserve soil moisture—the best way to reduce weeding.

Native plants: What would be growing everywhere here if Columbus hadn't arrived in America.

Organic gardening: A method of gardening using only materials derived from living things—garden tools excepted. For example, composts and manures instead of chemical fertilizers, and naturally occurring pesticides instead of synthetic ones.

Organic material: The stuff gardeners never have enough of. Any material (compost, manure, leaf mold) derived from a living organism.

Peat moss: The partially decomposed remains of mosses that are used as a soil conditioner or as the main ingredient in potting soil. So light you can impress clueless friends when you lift a whole bag by yourself.

Perennial: A non-woody (herbaceous) plant that grows and lives for more than two years if you haven't managed to kill it off in year one.

Pest: Any insect or animal that is detrimental to the health and well-being of plants. The passer-by who wants to chat but never helps out when you're weeding.

Photosynthesis: The process by which plants turn sunlight into food energy, which keeps them light years ahead of gardeners, who have to stop for breakfast, lunch, and dinner.

Pinching back: Using your thumb and forefinger or pruners to nip back the tip of a branch or stem to promote a bushier, fuller plant. What your spouse wants to do to you after you've gone overboard at the garden center.

Pruning: An occasional haircut plants, particularly woody ones, need. The process by which clueless gardeners turn shrubs into odd shapes like burgers and beer cans.

Root ball: The roots of plants and the soil that's attached—big root balls make moving good-sized trees a weighty business.

Root-bound: When a potted plant has outgrown its container and the roots become entangled. The gardener who has lived in one place for too long.

Runner: A slender stem growing from the base of some plants that terminates at a new offset (plant). Ideally, a person who fetches your spade, trowel, and garden gloves when you misplace them.

Soil pH: A fancy name for whether your soil is on acid or not.

Staking: Nothing to do with Buffy and Dracula, so relax—it's the practice of driving a stake into the ground to support an excessively relaxed plant.

Sucker: A growth originating from the rootstock rather than the desired part of a grafted plant. Also a new stem of a spready shrub.

Or the gardener who regularly gets distracted by pretty colors in the garden center and leaves with a much thinner wallet.

Tender plants: Plants that are unable to endure frost or freezing temperatures. Tender gardeners share this weakness.

Thinning: Removing excess seedlings to allow sufficient room for the remaining plants to grow. What you hope will happen to your midriff as a result of gardening.

Topsoil: The top layer of native soil or good-quality soil sold at garden suppliers. There never seems to be enough in your garden.

Transplanting: The process of digging up a plant and moving it to another location and moving it back because you've changed your mind.

Variegated: Leaves marked with multiple colors—plants that look good in stripes.

Zones of hardiness: Areas of similar temperatures and growing conditions. Most gardeners would transplant themselves to a warmer zone at the drop of a hat.

Resources: More Help for the New Gardener

Soil

Hynes, Erin. *Improving the Soil.* Emmaus, PA: Rodale Press, 1994.

Stell, Elizabeth P. *Secrets to Great Soil.* Pownal, VT: Storey Books, 1998.

Water-wise Gardening

Bennett, Jennifer. *Dry-Land Gardening.* Toronto: Firefly Books, 1998.

Lawns, Ground Covers, Ornamental Grasses, and Native Plants

Darke, Rick. *The Color Encyclopedia of Ornamental Grasses.* Portland, OR: Timber Press, 1999.

Gilmer, Maureen. *The Complete Idiot's Guide to a Beautiful Lawn.* New York: Alpha Books, 1999.

Johnson, Lorraine. *Grow Wild.* Toronto: Random House Canada, 1998.

MacKenzie, David S. *Perennial Ground Covers.* Portland, OR: Timber Press, 1997.

Otteson, Carole. *The Native Plant Primer.* New York: Harmony Books, 1995.

Flower Gardening

Armitage, Allan. *Armitage's Garden Perennials: A Colour Encyclopedia.* Portland, OR: Timber Press, 2000.

DiSabato-Aust, Tracy. *The Well-Tended Perennial Garden.* Portland, OR: Timber Press, 1998.

Hodgson, Larry. *Perennials for Every Purpose.* Emmaus, PA: Rodale Press, 2000.

Hogue, Marjorie Mason. *Amazing Annuals.* Toronto: Firefly Books, 1999.

Lima, Patrick. *The Art of Perennial Gardening.* Toronto: Firefly Books, 1998.

Shade Gardening

Druse, Ken. *The Natural Shade Garden.* New York: Clarkson Potter, 1992.

Schenk, George. *The Complete Shade Gardener.* Boston: Houghton Mifflin, 1984.

Schenk, George. *Moss Gardening: Including Lichens, Liverworts, and Other Miniatures.* Portland, OR: Timber Press, 1997.

Trees and Shrubs

Cole, Trevor. *Gardening with Trees and Shrubs*. Vancouver, BC: Whitecap Books, 1996.

Dirr, Michael A. *Dirr's Hardy Trees and Shrubs: An Illustrated Encyclopedia*. Portland, OR: Timber Press, 1997.

Osborne, Robert. *Hardy Trees and Shrubs: A Guide to Disease-Resistant Varieties for the North*. Toronto: Key Porter Books, 1996.

Zucker, Isabel. *Flowering Shrubs and Small Trees*. Revised and expanded by Derek Fell. Toronto: Stoddart 1990.

Web resource on tree care: Go to the International Society of Arboriculture's Web site at **www2.champaign.isa-arbor.com/sitemap.html** and click on "Tree Care Consumer Information."

Vegetable Gardening

Smith, Edward C. *The Vegetable Gardener's Bible*. Pownal, VT: Storey Books, 2000.

Solving Garden Problems

Grissell, Eric. *Insects and Gardens*. Portland, OR: Timber Press, 2001.

Olkowski, William, Sheila Darr, and Helga Olkowski. *The Gardener's Guide to Common-Sense Pest Control*. Newtown, CT: Taunton Press, 1995.

Rodale's All-New Encyclopedia of Organic Gardening. Edited by Fern Marshall Bradley and Barbara W. Ellis. Emmaus, PA: Rodale Press, 1997.

York, Karen. *The Holistic Garden: Creating Spaces for Health and Healing*. Toronto: Prentice Hall Canada, 2001.

Garden Design

Brookes, John. *Garden Masterclass*. London: DK Publishing, 2002.

Oudolf, Piet, with Noël Kingsbury. *Designing with Plants*. Portland, OR: Timber Press, 1999.

Pope, Nori, and Sandra Pope. *Color by Design*. San Francisco: Soma Books, 1998.

Garden Tools

Web resources

www.gardenerstoolbelt.com

www.leevalleytools.com

www.rittenhouse.ca

Index